Teen Health

COURSE 3

Student Activities Workbook
Teacher Annotated Edition

McGraw Hill Glencoe

Glencoe

The **McGraw·Hill** Companies

Printed in the United States of America.

Send all inquiries to:
Glencoe/McGraw-Hill
21600 Oxnard Street, Suite 500
Woodland Hills, California 91367

ISBN-13: 978-0-07-877475-1   (Student Activity Workbook)
MHID-10: 0-07-877475-6   (Student Activity Workbook)
ISBN-13: 978-0-07-877476-8   (Student Activity Workbook, TAE)
MHID-10: 0-07-877476-4   (Student Activity Workbook, TAE)

1 2 3 4 5 6 7 8 9 079 12 11 10 09 08
1 2 3 4 5 6 7 8 9 079 12 11 10 09 08

Table of Contents

Introduction

This Workbook contains Study Guides, Activities, Health Inventories, and Applying Health Skills activities to accompany the chapters in your student textbook. In addition, activities to help you master academic vocabulary terms related to mental and emotional health, disease prevention, injury prevention, and environmental health are provided beginning on page 169.

The Study Guides are to be completed as you read each lesson. They will help you check your understanding of lesson content. Each Study Guide consists of questions to help you outline the main ideas in the chapter. After you have completed all the questions, you can use the Study Guide to review the information in the chapter as a whole.

Following each Study Guide, there are Activities—one for each lesson in your textbook. The Activities give you opportunities to apply what you have learned. A variety of formats is offered, including fill-ins, short-answer, matching, classifying, and sequencing. In some Activities, you are asked to complete or analyze a chart, or to label a diagram.

A Health Inventory follows the Activities for each *odd* chapter. Each Health Inventory offers you an opportunity to assess your own health or health behaviors. The purpose of the Health Inventories is to help you recognize what you are doing that is good for your health and identify behaviors that you need to change.

An Applying Health Skills activity follows the Activities for each *even* chapter. Each Applying Health Skills activity gives you an opportunity to practice one of the ten health skills introduced in Chapter 2 of your text-book. These skills can help you stay healthy throughout your entire life.

Academic Vocabulary in the Health Classroom

Every content area has distinctive vocabulary words used to describe ideas and concepts that are unique to the subject or field of study. Such terms are known as **technical vocabulary**. In the study of health, words like *emphysema*, *diaphragm*, and *infection* are used to describe health conditions and human anatomy—concepts specific to health. Words that are considered technical vocabulary have only one meaning. These terms are often defined or explained within the *Teen Health* text.

In addition to the technical vocabulary words introduced within the *Teen Health* text, you will encounter another type of words known as **academic vocabulary**. Academic vocabulary is used in many different content areas. Words like *trigger* and *flexibility* have specific meanings when used within the context of health. In other content areas, meanings of these terms may differ. Other words, like *evaluate, interpret, enable,* and *strategy*, have the same meanings across content areas. Knowing and understanding academic vocabulary is important to developing strong reading and comprehension skills.

Chapter 1 Study Guide
Understanding Your Health

Study Tips
✔ Read the chapter objectives.
✔ Look up any unfamiliar words.
✔ Read the questions below before you read the chapter.

As you read the chapter, answer the following questions. Later you can use this guide to review the information in the chapter.

Lesson 1

1. What does it mean to be healthy?

   Being healthy means many things, including having a fit body, feeling well, feeling good

   about yourself, and getting along with others.

2. Name the three parts of the health triangle, and list two aspects of each side.

   The three parts of the health triangle are physical, mental/emotional, and social health.

   Two aspects of physical health include (any two): taking care of your body; eating a

   balanced food plan; being physically active; avoiding harmful behaviors; and visiting your

   doctors for regular checkups. Two aspects of mental/emotional health include (any two):

   liking and accepting yourself; expressing feelings and emotions in healthy ways; having a

   positive attitude; and handling stress and challenges. Two aspects of social health include

   (any two): getting along with others; caring and supporting friends and family members;

   communicating well; and showing respect.

3. Why is it important to keep your health triangle balanced?

   Keeping your health triangle balanced will make you a healthy person.

   _____

4. Explain why wellness is more than just being healthy.

   Wellness is an overall state of well-being, or total health. To achieve wellness, you need to

   make good health a part of your daily routine and make choices that promote good

   health now and in the future.

Chapter 1 Study Guide
Understanding Your Health

Lesson 2

5. Identify three characteristics of adolescence.

Three characteristics of adolescence include (any three): physical, mental/emotional, and social growth; a time when you make new friends; when you begin forming your own opinions and beliefs; when you try new activities or sports; and a time when you experience mood swings.

6. What are *hormones?*

Hormones are chemical substances, produced in glands, that help regulate many body functions.

7. List two changes that occur during adolescence for each of the following: physical growth, mental and emotional growth, and social growth.

Two physical growth changes that occur during adolescence include (any two): growing taller; growing body hair; boys' voices get deeper; girls may notice their figures developing; and hands and feet may grow faster than the rest of the body. Two mental and emotional growth changes that occur during adolescence include (any two): beginning to think and reason differently; thinking about the consequences of your actions; the ability to solve difficult problems; developing your own values and beliefs; experiencing mood swings; possibly experiencing feelings of attraction; and understanding the importance of the people in your life. Two social growth changes that occur during adolescence include (any two): making more choices and decisions; no longer depending on parents as much; friends and peers become very important; and beginning to recognize your role in the community.

8. Define *community service.*

Community service is involvement in volunteer programs whose goal is to improve the community and the life of its residents.

Chapter 1 Study Guide
Understanding Your Health

Lesson 3

9. What are lifestyle factors?

Lifestyle factors are behaviors and habits that help determine a person's level of health and wellness.

10. Identify three examples of positive lifestyle factors.

Any three of the following: Eating well-balanced meals, starting with a good breakfast; getting at least 60 minutes of physical activity daily; sleeping at least 8 hours every night; doing your best in school and at all activities you take on; avoiding tobacco, alcohol, and other drugs; following rules of safety and wearing protective gear; relating well to family, friends, and classmates.

11. Explain why a sendentary lifestyle is a risk behavior.

A sendentary lifestyle is a risk behavior because it is a way of life that includes little physical activity. Sitting in front of a computer or TV becomes a risk when it continually replaces sports or other physical activities.

12. Explain why abstinence from risk behaviors is a wise choice for teens.

Abstinence from risk behaviors is a wise choice for teens because it shows that you are responsible and that you respect yourself. Abstinence also benefits all three sides of your health triangle.

Activity 1
Use with Chapter 1, Lesson 1

The Signs of Good Health

Read the statements in the left column. If the statement describes good health, place a check next to it in the middle column. In the right column identify the type of health being described. Your choices are: physical health, mental/emotional health, and social health. Leave blank any statement that does not describe a sign of good health.

Descriptions		Type of Health
1. Tom has played both football and baseball for 5 years.	✔	physical
2. Jane gets along well with others and makes friends easily.	✔	social
3. John feels as though he has many faults and constantly worries about his mistakes.		
4. To help him relax, Jordan has the habit of taking long walks daily.	✔	mental/emotional
5. Fred smokes.		
6. Lisa gets regular checkups from medical professionals.	✔	physical
7. Ted handles stressful situations and challenges with a positive attitude.	✔	mental/emotional
8. When Andy has problems, he is unable to find solutions.		
9. Shannon is negative and critical toward others.		
10. Meg keeps her thoughts to herself and rarely expresses what she feels.		
11. Tim values and respects others.	✔	social
12. Jamie makes friends quickly, but does not keep them. He spends most of his free time alone.		
13. Sam refuses to spend time with his family.		
14. Martin eats healthy meals and enjoys cooking.	✔	physical
15. Each year Sean has intense conflict with at least three of his teachers.		

Activity 2
Use with Chapter 1, Lesson 2

Changes During the Teen Years

Read each question. Then, write the answer that you think a health care professional would give.

Question	Answer from a health care professional
1. What makes me so different?	You are realizing that all people are unique. You are wondering this because adolescence is a period of discovery. You are searching to discover things about yourself and your abilities.
2. Sometimes I want to stay a child. Why am I afraid to become an adult?	Several things about you are changing. It is natural to be concerned about all of these physical, social, and emotional changes. You are probably recognizing that with more independence comes more responsibility.
3. Both of my best friends look like young women. Why do I still look like a little girl?	Puberty does not begin at the same time for everyone.
4. Why do I feel so awkward, like my arms and legs do not belong to me any more?	Your hormones are changing, and your growth is uneven.
5. Sometimes I get so confused when I listen to people argue. I can see both points of view and cannot decide who is right.	You are able to think on a more complex level.
6. When I listen to people talk about politics, I find myself interested. I wonder why that is, since I never cared about politics before.	You are thinking more and developing your own values and beliefs.
7. Why do I feel happy one moment and sad the next?	You are experiencing mood swings that result from the release of hormones.
8. Why do I often think about what college I want to go to and what kind of job I want?	You have an increased awareness of what is important to you and that includes your goals and education. Your sense of responsibility is growing.

Activity 3
Use with Chapter 1, Lesson 3

Chapter 1

Taking Responsibility for Your Health

Imagine that you have been asked to create a display for the front hall in your school. The topic for the display is the positive consequences of following healthy behaviors.

The title for the display is "Healthy Behaviors."

In each of the flags below, you have been directed to include:

1. A healthy behavior

2. The benefit of the healthy behavior

The first one is done for you. Answers will vary.

Get enough sleep.
If you do, you will have the energy you will need.

Exercise daily.
You need physical activity to stay healthy.

Protect yourself from the harmful rays of the sun.
Sunburns and skin cancer are dangerous.

Never use drugs.
Drugs are emotionally and physically addictive. Drug use damages both health and relationships.

If your friend has a problem, listen.
People need to know someone cares.

Do not engage in sexual activity.
Emotionally, you are not ready, and you may get pregnant or a disease.

Do not try smoking.
Smoking, which is addictive, causes lung disease and cancer.

Chapter 1 Health Inventory

Your Total Health

Read the statements below. In the space at the left, write *yes* if the statement describes you, or *no* if it does not describe you.

_____ **1.** I accept constructive criticism when it is given.

_____ **2.** I feel comfortable when meeting new people.

_____ **3.** I get at least 8 hours of sleep a night.

_____ **4.** I eat a variety of healthy foods.

_____ **5.** I stay within 5 pounds of my appropriate weight range.

_____ **6.** I can accept other people's ideas and suggestions.

_____ **7.** I do 20 minutes or more of vigorous physical activity at least three times a week.

_____ **8.** I am happy most of the time.

_____ **9.** I can accept differences in people.

_____ **10.** I can say no to my friends if they are doing something I do not want to do.

_____ **11.** I have at least one or two close friends.

_____ **12.** I ask for help when I need it.

_____ **13.** I seldom feel tired or run-down.

_____ **14.** I can express my feelings to others in healthy ways.

_____ **15.** I can name at least three activities I perform well.

Score yourself:

Write the number of *yes* answers here. ☐

12–15: Your health practices are very good.

8–11: Your health practices are good.

5–7: Your health practices are fair.

Fewer than 5: Your health practices are in need of some changes.

Chapter 2 Study Guide
Skills for a Healthy Life

Study Tips
✔ Read the chapter objectives.
✔ Look up any unfamiliar words.
✔ Read the questions below before you read the chapter.

As you read the chapter, answer the following questions. Later you can use this guide to review the information in the chapter.

Lesson 1

1. Define *decision making* and explain the value of having decision-making skills.

Decision making is the process of making a choice or finding a solution. Decision-making

skills help you make the best choices and find healthful solutions to problems.

2. What are the six steps in the decision-making process?

State the situation; list the options; weigh the possible outcomes; consider your values;

make a decision and act; evaluate your decision.

3. Define *goal setting,* and explain the benefit of goal-setting skills.

Goal setting is the process of working toward something you want to accomplish.

Goal-setting skills help you control your life and give it purpose and direction.

4. Name the six steps of the goal-setting process.

Identify a specific goal and write it down. List the steps you will take to reach your goal.

Get help and support from others. Identify and overcome specific obstacles. Evaluate

your progress. Give yourself a reward once you have achieved your goal.

Lesson 2

5. Define *character*.

Character is the way in which a person thinks, feels, and acts. It involves caring about

and acting upon certain values.

Chapter 2 Study Guide
Skills for a Healthy Life

Chapter 2

6. What are the six main traits that work together to form good character?

The traits of good character are: trustworthiness, respect, responsibility, fairness, caring,

and citizenship.

7. Define *tolerance* and *prejudice*. Explain how the two words relate to
each other.

Tolerance is the ability to accept other people as they are. Prejudice is an opinion or

fear formed without having facts or firsthand knowledge. Tolerance can be a tool in

countering prejudice.

8. Give three examples of qualities found in caring people.

Any three: Caring people are kind. They show empathy, which is the ability to understand

and show concern for the feelings of others. They do not look for revenge. They forgive,

or try to forgive, those who hurt them. They give of themselves, sharing their time and

talent.

Lesson 3

9. Name the five health skills that relate to communication.

The life skills are: communication, accessing information, analyzing influences, refusal

skills, and conflict-resolution skills.

10. What does practicing healthful behaviors help you do?

Practicing healthful behaviors helps you balance your health triangle.

11. Define *stress*.

Stress is your body's response to change. Stress is a normal part of life. Two types of stress

are positive stress and challenging stress.

12. What are ways to manage stress?

Stress management can include relaxation and managing your time effectively.

Activity 4
Use with Chapter 2, Lesson 1

Chapter 2

Making Decisions and Setting Goals

Amber loves life and other people, but she feels like she makes one bad decision after another. She feels that sometimes her life lacks purpose even though she works hard and wants to do the right thing.

Read the following snapshot from Amber's life. After the snapshot, you will find charts for decision making and goal setting. Beside the steps on each chart, fill in what you think Amber should have done differently in the situation.

Snapshot of Amber

Amber is an outgoing, social teen. She loves to laugh and to have fun with others. Monday, during lunch, she announced that she is having a party that Friday night. All day people told her that they would come. Since she was not sure how many would attend her party, she ordered quantities of snacks and soda to be delivered on Friday morning. Then, she bought a new dress to wear. On Wednesday she spent the evening making up party games and activities. By Thursday she sat down with her mother to go over her party activities. Her mother was angry because her aunt and her six children were due to arrive Friday morning. Friday, Amber went to school in a bad mood because she had to tell everyone that the party was off.

The Decision-Making Process	What Amber should have done differently
Step 1: State the Situation	Amber needed to consider what would be the best possible plan for her party. She needed to consider who was involved instead of just picking a day.
Step 2: List the Options	She should have asked her mother if she could have a party and what dates would be best. She needed to make a list of who would attend.
Step 3: Weigh the Possible Outcomes	By determining which date would be the best for the people involved, Amber could avoid upsetting anyone.
Step 4: Consider Your Values	Amber needed to consider the value of respect by checking with her mother first.
Step 5: Make a Decision and Act	Once she had a date that suited others, she could begin preparations.
Step 6: Evaluate Your Decision	After the party, Amber should evaluate the activities she created.

Activity 4
Use with Chapter 2, Lesson 1

The Goal-Setting Process	What Amber should have done differently
Step 1: Identify a Specific Goal and Write It Down	Amber should have asked her parents if she could have a party at their home.
Step 2: List the Steps You Will Take to Reach Your Goal	She needed to organize her party plans by getting permission and listing guests, food, and activities.
Step 3: Get Help and Support from Others	Amber's mother may have helped, and her close friends probably would have made up the guest list.
Step 4: Identify and Overcome Specific Obstacles	The main obstacle seems to be finding a time that suits her mother.
Step 5: Evaluate Your Progress	With a list, Amber can check off names and preparation plans.
Step 6: Give Yourself a Reward Once You Have Achieved Your Goal	Amber would probably be rewarded by having fun at her party.

Activity 5
Use with Chapter 2, Lesson 2

Chapter 2

Building Good Character

At your school assembly this month, three people are being given "Good Character Awards." You are given the task of introducing each person. To prepare, you take notes about what each person has done to be given the "Good Character Award." In addition, you review the traits of good character that you learned in health class. They include: **trustworthiness, respect, responsibility, fairness, caring,** and **citizenship.**

Directions: Under the card with the notes about each person, write your introduction. Be sure to identify how the person's activities show the specific traits of good character.

Answers will vary, but should include much of the following:

1.

> **Fred**
>
> • Goes around the neighborhood collecting food and clothing for the local charities
>
> • Gets cash sometimes, but never keeps any of it
>
> • Takes turns going to all of the different charities around the area, so each charity gets its fair share

> **Your introduction of Fred:**
> Fred shows good citizenship and caring by helping people in the community, respect and fairness by rotating his deliveries, and trustworthiness with money.

2.

> **Mary**
>
> • Babysits for mothers in her neighborhood for an affordable fee
> • Rocks infants, reads stories to toddlers, takes youngsters on nature walks
> • Leaves the house clean with toys picked up
> • Does not allow kids to break rules

> **Your introduction of Mary:**
> Mary shows caring for others and respect for the families in her neighborhood.

Activity 5
Use with Chapter 2, Lesson 2

3.

> ### Cheryl
>
> - Volunteers at an after-school program in an elementary school
> - Plays games and reads to the children
> - Helps others with homework
> - Listens to problems, but never repeats what is said
> - Makes sure all of the children get attention and concern

> **Your introduction of Cheryl:**
>
> Cheryl is responsible and caring by really working and helping. She is fair as she gives attention to all of the children.

Chapter 2

Activity 6
Use with Chapter 2, Lesson 3

Developing Other Health Skills

Read the following statements that describe real-life situations. In the space on the left, write the health skill that could help solve the situation. On the line provided, write the question that should be asked to guide the situation.

Health Skills are:

Communication	Analyze Influences	Conflict Resolution	Advocacy
Access Information	Refusal Skills	Stress Management	

Answers will vary. Possible responses are provided.

Advocacy

1. Cars speed up and down the streets by the school. These streets are used by children who walk home.

   How can the community ensure the safety of the children?

Conflict Resolution

2. On every Saturday for the last two months, two sisters have gotten into an argument about what television show to watch. Both have ended up restricted to their rooms for the afternoon.

   What is a solution that would satisfy both girls?

Communication

3. Connor sits right behind Julie. He pops and smacks his gum all period. Julie is annoyed by him because she cannot pay attention.

   How can Julie communicate her feelings?

Access Information

4. Twelve people were taken out of their morning classes and sent home because they have head lice.

   How can you prevent having head lice?

Refusal Skills

5. Paige set up a plan that one of her friends would only do the math homework. Another friend would only do science, and so on. Then, everybody would copy from each other.

   How do you refuse the temptation to cheat?

Activity 6
Use with Chapter 2, Lesson 3

_____Communication_____

6. At the meeting, Jesse is sitting in complete silence with his arms folded.

What is Jesse's body language and silence communicating?

_____Analyze Influence_____

7. All of a sudden, Jill started wearing a new, fancy outfit every day.

What is influencing Jill to put so much importance on clothes?

_____Stress Management_____

8. Crystal's father got a new job, and she had to move to a different state.

How can Crystal deal with this change?

_____Stress Management_____

9. Erica is overwhelmed with pressure to get good grades, do well on the volleyball team, and write for the school newspaper.

What are some positive ways Erica can manage her stress?

_____Advocacy_____

10. A friend of yours at school was recently in a car accident. The other driver, who ran into him, was driving while intoxicated.

How can the community promote road safety and sober driving?

Applying Health Skills

Chapter 2

Stress Management

Your Body's Response to Change

Stress is your body's response to change. Some stress is positive and can give you energy. Other stress can be challenging.

Read each situation in the chart below. Write the cause(s) of the stress in the second column. Then write the stress-management technique that could help each teen. Answers will vary. Possible responses provided.

Situation	Cause(s) of Stress	Stress-Management Technique
1. Christopher has put off starting his science project until the night before it is due. Now it is 10:00 and he is tired, in a panic, and does not even know where to begin.	Science project is due in the morning.	Christopher could break the science project into smaller parts; he might also ask for help from his family.
2. Megan has been hearing her parents fight at night after she goes to bed. She is worried that they are going to get a divorce. As a result, she has not been able to eat lately and is losing weight.	Megan is worried about her parents fighting.	She could talk to her parents about what she is hearing. She could also speak to a school counselor about her concerns.
3. During the winter, Justin broke his leg skiing. Unable to get physical activity for a period of time, he gained weight. Now that the cast is off, and he is able to move again, he is worried that his weight gain will keep him from making the baseball team.	Justin is worried that his weight gain will keep him from making the baseball team.	Justin could begin a weight-management program to return to his healthful weight. He could also ask his baseball coach for suggestions about getting back in shape for the baseball season.
4. Amanda has changed schools in the middle of the year and is having a hard time making new friends. She had been an excellent student in her previous school, but she is having a hard time adjusting to her new surroundings and is now failing math.	Amanda started a new school in the middle of the year and has not made friends yet. She is now failing math.	Amanda could try to make new friends so that her adjustment to her new school is easier. She could ask for extra help from her math teacher.

Chapter 3 Study Guide
Mental and Emotional Health

Study Tips

✔ Read the chapter objectives.

✔ Look up any unfamiliar words.

✔ Read the questions below before you read the chapter.

As you read the chapter, answer the following questions. Later you can use this guide to review the information in the chapter.

Lesson 1

1. Name four signs of good mental and emotional health.

Four signs of good mental and emotional health include (any four): you accept that

things may not always go the way you plan; you set and achieve goals; you cope with

your feelings in healthy ways; you accept constructive or helpful feedback; and you

express your feelings through your words and creative outlets.

2. What influences your self-concept?

Your experiences, relationships, and people, such as friends, family members, teachers,

classmates, and coaches, influence your self-concept.

3. How can you improve your mental and emotional health?

You can improve your mental and emotional health by listing your strengths,

remembering that everyone makes mistakes, and by motivating yourself.

Lesson 2

4. Describe the feeling of jealousy.

Jealousy is resentment or unhappiness at another's good fortune.

5. What is the difference between anxiety and panic?

Anxiety is a state of uneasiness, usually associated with a future uncertainty, whereas

panic is a feeling of sudden, intense fear.

Chapter 3 Study Guide
Mental and Emotional Health

Chapter 3

6. How can you meet your three emotional needs?

You can meet the need to love and be loved by caring about and offering encouragement to friends and family members. You can meet the need to belong by joining clubs or groups at school and spending time with your family. You can meet the need to feel like you are making a difference by volunteering, doing community service, and setting goals for yourself.

Lesson 3

7. What is a *stressor*?

A stressor is anything that causes stress.

8. What does your body release during the fight-or-flight response?

Your body releases adrenaline.

9. Name three relaxation techniques that can help manage stress.

Three relaxation techniques that can help manage stress are taking deep slow breaths, getting plenty of sleep, and laughing.

Lesson 4

10. Define *grief reaction*.

Grief reaction is the process of dealing with strong feelings following any loss.

11. Describe the depression stage of a grief reaction.

In the depression stage, you realize the size of your loss, and deep sadness sets in.

12. What are coping strategies?

Coping strategies are ways of dealing with the sense of loss people feel at the death of someone close.

Activity 7
Use with Chapter 3, Lesson 1

Your Mental and Emotional Health

People with good mental and emotional health have a positive outlook on life, accept themselves and others, and adapt to new situations. **Personality, self-concept,** and **self-esteem** are factors related to mental and emotional health.

Read the descriptions below. Then, write the factor being described in the space provided.

1. The unique combination of feelings, thoughts, and behaviors that make you different from everyone else is your _____personality_____.

2. _____Self-concept_____ is described as positive or negative.

3. _____Self-concept_____ can stand in the way of setting goals if it is negative.

4. _____Self-esteem_____ can be high or low.

5. How much you value yourself is your _____self-esteem_____.

6. _____Self-esteem_____ can be increased by listing strengths.

7. Some people have a shy _____personality_____ while others do not.

8. The view you have of yourself is your _____self-concept_____.

9. Your _____self-concept_____ is healthy if you can accept that you make mistakes sometimes and can learn from them and move on.

10. You feel valued and appreciated when your _____self-esteem_____ is high.

11. When you are disappointed, you can bounce back emotionally, or show resilience, if your _____self-esteem_____ is high.

12. Your _____self-concept_____ can become more positive when you accomplish work.

13. The way you believe others see you affects your _____self-concept_____.

14. Your positive _____self-concept_____ gives you the confidence to work toward goals and achieve them.

15. Your _____self-concept_____ can be influenced in a positive or negative way in response to actions and remarks made by family, teachers, and other important people in your life.

Activity 8

Use with Chapter 3, Lesson 2

Emotions

Emotions show how you feel. They can be expressed in healthy or unhealthy ways. Emotions can serve a positive or a negative function in your life.

Describe the positive side, the negative side, and a healthy way to express each of the emotions identified below.

The Good Side

Understanding Anger

The good side is it is an emotional release to the frustrations of life. The bad side is anger can make the situation worse. The best way to express anger is to wait until you relax and then tell the other person calmly how you feel and what has caused you to feel this way.

The Bad Side

The Good Side

Understanding Anxiety

The good side is it gets the body ready for action and increases energy levels. The bad side of anxiety is when it builds up it can interfere with the normal functions of life. You should express anxiety by talking through problems, sharing feelings, and meeting challenges head-on.

The Bad Side

The Good Side

Understanding Fear

The good side of fear is that it is an alarm system that keeps you safe and prepares you for quick action. However, fear can keep you from doing things that you need to do. A healthy way to express fear is to talk about your fears to family and friends.

The Bad Side

Activity 9
Use with Chapter 3, Lesson 3

Stress Management

Imagine that you represent a counseling service. You have been given the job of writing "infomercials," telling people how your counseling service can help them deal with the stressors of life. An infomercial is a commercial that provides information and expresses a specific viewpoint.

Write infomercials for any three stressors listed below.

<u>List of Stressors</u>

Taking a test

Playing in a championship game

Living with an annoying family member

Changing schools

Being chased almost every day by the vicious dog who lives next door

Getting into an argument with a long-time friend

Finding out a friend has been talking about you in a mean way

Your infomercials must include:

1. A description of the stressor
2. What can happen if people do not deal with this stressor in a healthy way
3. Solutions that your counseling service will help people use
   Answers will vary but should include the following:

> 1. Excessive stress causes health problems, makes you emotionally unstable and unable to work or have fun, and leads to social withdrawal or outbursts toward others.

> 2. Ways to deal with stress include relaxing, maintaining a positive outlook, staying physically active, managing time, talking to family and friends, and resting more than usual.

Chapter 3

Activity 10
Use with Chapter 3, Lesson 4

Stages of Grief

When someone you know suffers a loss, you can help by understanding the person's emotional needs. One way to do this is to recognize the person's stage in the grief process. Often, the best thing you can do is to just be there, listen, and understand, allowing the grieving person to express what he or she needs.

Read the following descriptions of people who have suffered a loss. Write the stage of grief they are in and an appropriate thing you could say.

The comments will vary, but should be within the following guidelines:

1. Manuel's grandmother has just died. He keeps saying that he cannot believe his grandmother is really gone.

   Stage: _____Denial_____

   > They should show understanding of the person's feelings. The person's feelings are not in any way wrong.

2. Jared was told that he did not make the football team. He is blaming his father, saying that his father did not teach him to pass the ball correctly.

   Stage: _____Anger_____

   > The person's feelings should be respected and not dismissed.

3. Nicole's father has cancer. Nicole shares all of the details about his treatments and the changes in her family's life. She tries very hard to help out at home, hoping it will help her father get better.

   Stage: _____Bargaining_____

   > The person should be asked what he or she needs, and what you can do to help.

4. Ali had a long, intense argument with her best friend Erica. Ali said things that she regrets—things Erica told her were unforgivable. Now Erica is not speaking to her, and Ali is deeply sad.

   Stage: _____Depression_____

   > Advice should not be given. Listen if the person wants to talk.

Chapter 3

Chapter 3 Health Inventory

Rate Your Mental and Emotional Total Health

Read the statements below. In the space at the left, write *yes* if the statement describes you, or *no* if it does not describe you.

_____ 1. I am interested in other people.

_____ 2. I face my problems rather than avoid them.

_____ 3. I can laugh at myself.

_____ 4. I know my limits as well as my abilities.

_____ 5. I like who I am.

_____ 6. I see challenges as opportunities for growth.

_____ 7. I set realistic goals for myself.

_____ 8. I am satisfied with my effort if I have done my best.

_____ 9. I can cope with disappointment.

_____ 10. I can give and accept compliments.

_____ 11. I am comfortable about expressing my feelings.

_____ 12. I continue to participate in an activity even if I do not always get my way.

_____ 13. I can say no to people without feeling guilty.

_____ 14. I enjoy my own company.

_____ 15. I can ask for help when I need it.

Score yourself:

How many *yes* answers did you have? Write the number here.

12–15: You have excellent mental and emotional health.

8–11: Your mental and emotional health is good.

5–7: Your mental and emotional health is fair, but it could be better.

Fewer than 5: Reread Chapter 3 carefully to see what changes you can make to improve your mental and emotional health.

Chapter 4 Study Guide
Mental and Emotional Problems

Chapter 4

> ## Study Tips
> ✔ Read the chapter objectives.
> ✔ Look up any unfamiliar words.
> ✔ Read the questions below before you read the chapter.

   As you read the chapter, answer the following questions. Later you can use this guide to review the information in the chapter.

Lesson 1

1. What are some characteristics of panic disorder?

   A person may sweat and tremble. His or her heart may pound. He or she may have

   shortness of breath or nausea or a fear of losing control.

   _____

   _____

2. What is a phobia? Name two examples of phobias.

   A phobia is an exaggerated fear of a specific situation or object. Two examples of

   phobias are fear of spiders and fear of crowded places.

   _____

3. What are some characteristics of borderline personality disorder?

   A person may have a hard time with close relationships with other people. He or she

   might idealize a person and lash out in anger or violence if disappointed by that person.

   He or she may also engage in high-risk behaviors, suffer from poor self-esteem, and

   have a fear of abandonment.

   _____

4. How can schizophrenia be treated?

   Schizophrenia can be treated with medication.

Chapter 4 Study Guide
Mental and Emotional Problems

Lesson 2

5. What is *suicide?*

Suicide is a leading cause of death among teens. It is the intentional taking of one's own life.

6. How are depression and suicide related?

Being depressed can lead to thoughts of suicide.

7. What are some examples of self-destructive behaviors that could be warning signs of suicide?

A sudden fascination with the topic of death, dramatic changes in the person's appearance, self-destructive behavior, withdrawal from friends, family, and regular activities.

8. What are some things to remember if you are ever thinking about suicide?

Suicide is never a solution to your problems. Feelings of depression do not last forever. You are not alone. Talk to someone close to you. There are organizations out there that can help you.

Lesson 3

9. List some adults a teen might be able to trust and talk to about his or her mental or emotional problems.

Answers will vary but may include the following: a parent, guardian, older sibling, school nurse, school counselor, teacher, coach, psychologist, clinical social worker, or psychiatrist.

10. What is *therapy?*

Therapy is an approach that teaches you different ways of thinking or behaving.

11. What is *family therapy?*

Family therapy is counseling that seeks to improve troubled family relationships.

12. What is a *clinical social worker?*

A clinical social worker is a licensed, certified mental health professional with a master's degree in social work.

Chapter 4

Activity 11
Use with Chapter 4, Lesson 1

Mental and Emotional Disorders

Read the following descriptions of people who have mental and emotional disorders. On the line provided, write the diagnosis from the box that is being described.

Panic Disorder	Borderline Personality Disorder
Obsessive-Compulsive Disorder	Schizophrenia
Post-Traumatic Stress Disorder	Bipolar Disorder
Phobia	Depression
Passive-Aggressive Personality Disorder	

1. Ann cannot step on cracks on the floor or on the sidewalk. When people try to force her to put her foot on a crack, she becomes intensely fearful and screams. She is irritable and tense most of the time.

   Phobia
   _____

2. John goes to the emergency room frequently with shortness of breath and trembling. He believes he is having a heart attack.

   Panic Disorder
   _____

3. Kayla has a difficult time cooperating with people. She complains about teachers, saying that they boss her around. She admits that she has not finished one assignment all term. At home she gets very angry when her parents punish her. Although she refuses to go any-where with her family, she accuses them of leaving her out of things.

   Passive-Aggressive Personality Disorder
   _____

4. Will hears voices. He is so distracted by these voices that he does not listen to what is actually said in class. Will does not say much to any-one, and admits that he does not trust people at all.

   Schizophrenia
   _____

5. Sometimes Katherine talks constantly in a loud voice. She is unable to sit still and annoys everyone by walking around touching every-thing in sight. Other times, Katherine stays in bed all day. She insists that her life is hopeless.

   Bipolar Disorder
   _____

Activity 12
Use with Chapter 4, Lesson 2

Suicide

Place a check mark beside every statement that could be a warning sign of suicide.

1. Sue believes her life is worthless.	✔
2. Jan is not depressed.	
3. Tim has a positive outlook on his future.	
4. Ann feels a strong connection to her family and friends. She appreciates their support.	
5. Sam says things like, "No one cares if I live or die."	✔
6. Kelsey is extremely careful not to engage in any risky behaviors and will not do anything that might hurt her.	
7. Juan has withdrawn from all his friends and does not take part in any of the activities that he used to enjoy.	✔
8. Alexandra says that she could care less about what she looks like, or if she ever goes out with people she knows again.	✔
9. Andy talks about death, writes about death, and asks people odd questions about death.	✔
10. Natalie believes that if she tries her best, even if she sometimes fails, she will be happy.	
11. Cameron knows that he has made mistakes in school lately, but he says he has learned from the mistakes and will do better next term.	
12. Stephanie gave away all of her jewelry and cute clothes, telling people that they could remember her when they wore her things.	✔
13. After months of being deeply depressed and hardly talking to anyone, Evan suddenly became cheerful and seemed like he knew what he wanted.	✔

Chapter 4

Activity 13
Use with Chapter 4, Lesson 3

Mental Health Questions

Imagine that you are a licensed clinical social worker who answers questions once a week on a radio talk show. People call in with questions about mental and emotional disorders. The topic this week is: "Should I be worried if …?" You will listen to the symptoms the caller describes and determine if he or she has a serious problem.

Read what the caller says and write *Yes* on the line if the caller has a serious problem and *No* if the caller does not. Then, write a sentence that states the reason for your response.

What the caller said:	Should the caller be worried?	Your reason:
1. "During the last months, I've stopped eating regular meals because I'm never hungry. I stay awake most of the night, walking around the house. I'm failing some of my classes at school. I feel nervous all the time."	Yes	Feelings of anxiety are affecting sleep, eating habits, and school-work.
2. "My therapist has recommended that I join his therapy group one night a week. He claims that the other people in the group will understand my problem and help me think of solutions."	No	Group therapy is a good idea. It can be reassuring because group members have similar problems and support each other.
3. "I have felt suicidal for the last year and do not like leaving my house. I stopped going to counseling because my aunt has told me that as long as I took my medication, I did not need to discuss my problems."	Yes	You need therapy to get to the root of your problems. You need to talk to someone who cares.
4. "I have not told anyone that I sleep most of the day. I have stopped speaking to my parents and my friends. There's no point in going to school since I'm failing anyway."	Yes	You have a serious problem that is affecting all areas of your life.
5. "I was given medication by my doctor for a chemical imbalance. I stopped taking them because I don't want to be on drugs."	Yes	Medications correct imbalances in the brain.
6. "I argue with my mother every day. Our family doctor has set up family therapy for us. I know I will be expected to talk about my feelings."	No	You need family therapy and you need to express your feelings.

Chapter 4

Applying Health Skills

Decision Making

How to Help A Friend

Read the following paragraph. Then, imagine you are Matt's friend. Applying the decision-making skills to the situation, fill in the six steps in the decision-making strategy that you would use to help Matt.

When Matt heard last month that his family would be moving across the country at the end of the school year, he was excited. Now, however, he seems depressed and does not want to talk about the move. Nothing that used to interest him seems to make him happy anymore. When you suggest an activity, he says, "I don't care." You are worried about Matt's mental health. You feel he may be showing some of the warning signs of suicide, but you are afraid to talk to him about it.

Apply the decision-making skills to Matt's situation and demonstrate how you would help your friend.
Answers will vary. Possible responses provided.

1. State the situation.

Matt seems depressed and is exhibiting possible suicidal signs.

2. List the options.

The options are to speak to Matt about his feelings and to speak to a trusted adult or

professional about the situation.

3. Weigh the possible outcomes.

If the friend speaks to Matt or speaks to a trusted adult or professional, there is more of a

chance that Matt could get help.

4. Consider your values.

The friend should consider what it means to be a true friend.

5. Make a decision and act.

The friend should talk to a trusted adult or professional.

6. Evaluate the decision.

The friend will know the decision was a positive one if Matt gets help for his depression.

Chapter 4

Chapter 5 Study Guide
Relationships: The Teen Years

Study Tips

✔ Read the chapter objectives.

✔ Look up any unfamiliar words.

✔ Read the questions below before you read the chapter.

As you read the chapter, answer the following questions. Later you can use this guide to review the information in the chapter.

Lesson 1

1. What does sympathetic mean?

Sympathetic is being aware of how you may be feeling at a given moment.

_____

2. What is peer pressure?

Peer pressure is the influence to go along with the beliefs and actions of other people

your age.

3. What should a dating relationship be based on?

Answers may vary but should include: Like any relationship, a dating relationship should

be based on caring and respect.

Lesson 2

4. What is communication?

Communication is the exchange of thoughts, feelings, and beliefs between two or

more people.

5. What is an "I" message, and why is it effective?

An "I" message is a statement that presents a situation from the speaker's personal

viewpoint. It is effective in that it does not accuse or attack the way that "you" messages

do. "I" messages tell what needs to be done. "I need you to wait for me," is more

effective than, "You didn't wait for me!"

Chapter 5 Study Guide
Relationships: The Teen Years

6. What is active listening?

Active listening is hearing, thinking about, and responding to the other person's message.

Lesson 3

7. What is indirect peer pressure?

Indirect peer pressure is more subtle than direct peer pressure. A person may do some-thing or act a certain way because he or she thinks it will make him or her fit in with the group.

8. In what ways can peer pressure be positive?

It can inspire you, encourage you to get involved in new activities or try new things, influence you to care more about your health and well-being, and motivate others who see your efforts.

9. What are refusal skills, and what can they help you do?

Refusal skills are communication strategies that help you say no effectively. Using your refusal skills will help you to stand by your values and keep your self-respect.

Lesson 4

10. What are consequences?

Consequences are outcomes or effects that may occur as a result of a decision or an action.

11. What is abstinence?

Abstinence is the conscious, active choice not to participate in high-risk behaviors.

12. Who can you talk to if you need help managing sexual feelings?

Answers will vary, but may include the following: You can talk to a trusted adult, such as a parent, coach, teacher, or counselor.

Chapter 5

Activity 14
Use with Chapter 5, Lesson 1

Send a Greeting

Teens sometimes use greeting cards to express their feelings. Imagine that you have become a creator of greeting cards.

Select any 2 of the topics listed below and create a greeting card for each. Draw the cover of the card and write the message that would go inside.

1. A good-bye card for a friend who is moving away
2. An appreciation card for a good friend
3. A sympathy card for a person who got in trouble because he was influenced by negative peer pressure
4. A celebration card for your friend whose team won the championship
5. An apology card to a dear friend

Answers will vary.

Chapter 5

Activity 15
Use with Chapter 5, Lesson 2

Communication Skills

Read the descriptions of conversations in the first column. Then complete the chart with the communication skill being used.

Using body language as an aid	Expressing a clear message
Using intonation to send a message	Mirroring what was said
Active listening	Using an "I" message
Using a "conversation encourager"	

Conversation	Communication Skill
1. The speaker uses a firm tone of voice.	Using intonation to send a message
2. The listener responds, "Wow, then what happened?"	Using a "conversation encourager"
3. The speaker opens his arms and smiles.	Using body language as an aid
4. The speaker says, "I am angry because I heard that you were talking about me."	Using an "I" message
5. The speaker maintains eye contact with the person to whom he is speaking.	Using body language as an aid
6. When the speaker paused, the listener said, "I understand that you believe Fred is in danger."	Mirroring what was said
7. The listener paid careful attention to what was said and nodded his head from time to time.	Active listening
8. The speaker said, "I am sure there has been a mistake and I do not owe you money."	Expressing a clear message

Chapter 5

Activity 16
Use with Chapter 5, Lesson 3

Benefit or Danger?

Complete the chart below by defining each term and identifying either the benefit or the danger of the term. The first term is done for you.

Term	Definition	Benefit	Danger
1. Positive Peer Pressure	A force that influences you to do what is right or to do your best, so you will be accepted by your peer group	It helps people by motivating them to do what is right or beneficial for them.	
2. Negative Peer Pressure	Negative peer pressure is a force that influences you to do what is wrong or what is harmful, so you will be accepted by your peer group.		The danger is the trouble or harm that results.
3. Refusal Skills	Refusal skills are communication strategies that help you say no effectively. They help you avoid doing something you don't want to do.	The greatest benefit is you gain self-respect and earn respect for your strength.	
4. S.T.O.P. Strategy	S.T.O.P. strategy is to say no in a firm voice, tell why not, offer other ideas, and promptly leave if all else fails.	The benefit is it is a way to say no clearly and earn respect.	
5. Aggressive	Aggressive communication is speaking in a forceful and hostile way.		The danger is that it stirs anger in the listener and can cause a fight.
6. Passive	Passive communication gives in without standing up for rights or needs.		The danger is the weakness it suggests.
7. Assertive	Assertive communication is speaking with confidence and clearly stating your intentions.	The benefit is the respect it gains and gives others.	
8. "Lines"	"Lines" are phrases that are used to convince someone.		They are dangerous because they are a form of negative peer pressure.

Chapter 5 (side tab)

Activity 17
Use with Chapter 5, Lesson 4

Healthful Behaviors

List as many benefits as you can find for each of the following concepts.

Concept	Benefits
1. Rules	Rules bring a sense of order and purpose to life.
2. Limits, Invisible Boundaries	Limits are invisible boundaries that protect and govern people.
3. Consequences	Consequences are the outcomes of actions that reinforce good choices or punish bad ones.
4. Sexual Abstinence	Sexual abstinence protects people from the risk of disease and unplanned pregnancy.
5. Affection without Sexual Intimacy	Affection shows you care, deepens bonds, displays character, and gives joy.
6. Delaying Parenthood until Adulthood	Delaying parenthood gives you time to discover yourself, achieve goals, and become financially and emotionally ready.

Chapter 5

Chapter 5 Health Inventory

Rate Your Relationships

Read the statements below. In the space at the left, write *yes* if the statement describes you, or *no* if it does not describe you.

_____ **1.** I always try to be myself.

_____ **2.** My friends and I respect each other's opinions.

_____ **3.** My friends know that I care about them.

_____ **4.** I express affection in healthy ways.

_____ **5.** My friends and I trust each other.

_____ **6.** I am sympathetic when bad things happen to my friends.

_____ **7.** My friends and I can depend on one another.

_____ **8.** I try to have a positive influence on my friends and peers.

_____ **9.** I am able to make new friends.

_____ **10.** I try to plan fun, safe activities with my friends.

_____ **11.** I use refusal skills to avoid negative peer pressure.

_____ **12.** I enjoy activities in a mixed group setting.

_____ **13.** If I have dating relationships, they are based on caring and respect.

_____ **14.** I understand the qualities of a good friend, and I always try to show them.

_____ **15.** I know that no one is perfect, and I can forgive a friend's mistakes.

Score yourself:

How many *yes* answers did you circle? Write the number here. ☐

11–15: You deserve top honors for your good friend and peer relationships.

6–10: You have average relationships with your friends and peers.

Fewer than 6: Changing some of your actions will allow you to have more valuable relationships with your friends and peers.

Chapter 6 Study Guide
Promoting Social Health

Study Tips

✔ Read the chapter objectives.

✔ Look up any unfamiliar words.

✔ Read the questions below before you read the chapter.

As you read the chapter, answer the following questions. Later you can use this guide to review the information in the chapter.

Lesson 1

1. What is social health, and what is its foundation?

   Social health is your ability to get along with the people around you. The foundation of

   social health is the relationships you form with other people.

2. What is a role, and what are some of the different roles teens play?

   A role is a part you play when you interact with another person. Teens often play the

   role of daughter, son, student, friend, teammate, and neighbor.

3. In what ways can you show respect in your relationships?

   You can be polite, and use good manners. You can be tolerant of the views of others.

   You can listen to others when they speak and not interrupt.

4. In what ways can you show trust in your relationships?

   You can be honest, loyal, and reliable. You can live up to your word, and keep your

   promises.

Lesson 2

5. What is a single-parent family?

   A single-parent family is a family made up of one parent plus a child or children.

6. What is an extended family?

   An extended family is a family in which one or more parents and children live with other

   relatives such as grandparents, aunts, uncles, and cousins.

Chapter 6

Chapter 6 Study Guide
Promoting Social Health

7. What are some of the ways families provide for social needs?

Families teach effective communication skills, good manners, and positive values.

They also teach and share cultural traditions.

8. What are some ways families change due to circumstances?

Sometimes families move to a new home in a new city or town. This can be stressful

for teens who have to adjust to a new school and make new friends. A family can also

experience financial problems, especially if a parent loses a job. This might cause the

family to cut spending, or cause teens to earn their own spending money. Serious

illness can bring about change. Teens may be asked to help out by caring for a sick

person or by taking on some of the responsibilities of the parent.

Lesson 3

9. What is a commitment, and why is marriage such a large commitment?

A commitment is a pledge or promise. Marriage is a long-term commitment. It is a legal

and social commitment between two people. It is a promise to care for, respect, and live

with each other for the rest of your lives.

10. What is a divorce?

A divorce is a legal end to a marriage contract.

11. What are some of the responsibilities of parenthood?

Answers will vary but may include the following points: Parents must set fair limits.

Parents must teach values and provide support, and act as good role models. They must

show fairness, trust, caring, and respect so their children learn from their example. Parents

must provide patience and unconditional love. They must also be calm and forgiving.

12. What are some health risks that can affect babies born from
teen mothers?

Babies born from teen mothers have a higher risk of premature delivery and a higher

risk of low birth weight. Low birth weight can lead to childhood health problems.

Chapter 6

Activity 18
Use with Chapter 6, Lesson 1

Healthy Relationships

Healthy relationships are built on the characteristics of:

1. Trust
2. Respect
3. Patience
4. Tolerance
5. Caring
6. Meeting the responsibilities of the role that you play in a relationship

Read the statements that describe healthy relationships. Beside each, write the characteristic(s) being described.

_____Patience_____ 1. George accepts Marge's tendency to be late. He sits quietly and reads a magazine while he waits.

_____Trust_____ 2. Sam knows that Jill will return the books that she is borrowing today, just as she has in the past.

_____Tolerance or Respect_____ 3. When Jake goes to Kim's house, he leaves his shoes neatly in the hall by the front door, in the same way that all of the members of Kim's family leave their shoes.

Caring, Tolerance, or Respect 4. When Matt does not eat sweets during the fasting period of his religion, Dan does not eat any sweets in front of Matt.

_____Respect_____ 5. Courtney is careful not to interrupt Alyssa when she is speaking.

Meeting responsibilities 6. Jordan is a writer for the school newspaper. He makes it a point to hand in his articles on time so that they can be edited before the deadline.

_____Respect_____ 7. Andy's photography teacher, who is Andy's best friend's older brother, just graduated from college and started teaching. Andy calls his teacher Mr. Sans, even though Mr. Sans is young, and Andy has known him for years.

_____Trust_____ 8. Becky has never once repeated any of the private thoughts that her best friend Beth shares with her.

Chapter 6

Activity 19
Use with Chapter 6, Lesson 2

Families

Is this family getting along? At the end of each description, answer *Yes* or *No*. Then, give the reason for your view.

Description of a Family	Yes or No?	Your Reason
1. All of the family members help to take care of their elderly grandmother.	Yes	Family members provide care for and look after each other.
2. Neither parent in this family cooks or shops for nutritious food, so the children just eat whatever snacks are around the house.	No	Parents must provide nutrition for the children and teach their children healthy habits.
3. Sasha and her mother are the only members of this family. They rarely have a conversation. Sasha feels as though her mother doesn't care about her.	No	Sasha's emotional needs are not being met by her mother.
4. Jerry and his dad are the only members of this family. Every evening, over dinner, Jerry and his dad discuss their days at school and work.	Yes	Jerry's dad is teaching him how to communicate and providing emotional security.
5. Whenever Gavin's dad is in a bad mood, he yells at Gavin.	No	Gavin's dad is not teaching him how to communicate effectively.
6. Cindy's mother and father work all day. Cindy refuses to babysit her younger sister after school, even though her parents expect her to.	No	Cindy is not meeting her responsibilities at home.
7. After Fran's mom died, Fran and her father met with the counselor at their church for support.	Yes	Major life changes are often helped by going to counseling.
8. After Trent's father lost his job, Trent had no money to go to the mall. His mother's paycheck was just enough to buy food and pay the bills.	Yes	Trent is being provided for.
9. Two years after Ann's parents divorced, Ann's mother remarried. Her new husband moved in with his daughter. Now Ann is willing to share her room with her new stepsister.	Yes	Changes like this do occur in families. However, during this difficult period, the members of this new family should discuss their feelings honestly.
10. Matt's dad, a member of the National Guard, has been called into active duty and sent to the Middle East. Now, Matt has to do far more chores around the house.	Yes	Change often brings more responsibility.

Activity 20
Use with Chapter 6, Lesson 3

Successful Marriage and Family Life

Read version A and version B of the same situation. Then, decide which version shows the more successful marriage and family. Write the version you prefer and three reasons this version is better on the lines below.

1. Monday morning with Amy and Rod

Version A	Version B
The alarm rings and both Amy and Rod get out of bed and go downstairs. Amy fixes coffee and a quick breakfast while Rod packs lunches for both of them. While they eat, they quietly discuss which bills they will pay. While Rod is dressing for work, Amy puts chicken and vegetables in a crock pot, so dinner will be ready when they get home, and they'll have time to watch a movie together. While Amy gets ready, Rod pays the bills that they agreed to pay. Then, he starts the car, so it will be warm for Amy. Together, looking forward to the evening, they leave for work.	The alarm rings and Amy gets up. She goes downstairs and fixes coffee and a quick breakfast while Rod continues to sleep. She calls to him, but he ignores her. She returns upstairs, calls a few more times, and finally starts getting ready for work. When she returns to the bedroom, he still is not up. She starts yelling, telling him how lazy he is. Rod finally gets up, and Amy goes downstairs. She is too upset to eat, so she decides to pay bills and discovers someone has spent extra money. When she goes back upstairs, yelling again, both lie and say the other spent the money on expensive lunches. Both leave for work without saying good-bye.

Version A is the better situation because Amy and Rod respect each other. They work together as a team.

Chapter 6

Activity 20

Use with Chapter 6, Lesson 3

2. Watching television with Barbara, Dan, and their three sons

Version A	Version B

Version A

Dan cooks dinner while Barbara watches television with the boys. The boys are fighting, and Barbara is yelling at them to stop. Finally, Dan joins them, but he is in a bad mood because the boys will not eat. Dan decides to watch the news, but cannot hear it because the youngest boy is whining and the other two are teasing him. The oldest boy remembers that he has homework, but says that he is too tired. Dan is too tired to argue, so he finds a program they all like. Barbara cannot watch though because the kitchen is a mess and no laundry is sorted. While Dan carries the sleeping younger boys up to bed, Barbara is left downstairs complaining and miserable. To avoid a fight, Dan ignores her and goes to bed.

Version B

The boys are seated at the kitchen table doing their homework while Barbara and Dan fix dinner. Dan helps his oldest son with his assignment, and the other boys take turns giving each other spelling checks. Finally, all homework is done and Barbara serves dinner. The house rule is that the television does not go on until all homework is completed, everyone has eaten, and all chores are done. Dan wants to watch the news, so he cleans the kitchen while Barbara and the boys sort laundry. The boys bring their own clothes up to their rooms, so they can watch their favorite program that comes on after the news. Before going to bed, each member of the family shares one thing about his or her day.

Version B is better because the family has rules that they follow, parents that support each other, and love is expressed.

Applying Health Skills

Communication Skills

Family Communication

Directions: With other students, take turns using and evaluating good communication skills in family conversations.

1. Form a group with two other students. Each of you will participate in two different conversations and observe one conversation.

2. When it is your turn to participate in a conversation, choose one of these topics. Circle the topic you and your partner have chosen. (You will do this twice, once with each of the other students in your group.)
   - A day my brother needed my help
   - Something I did for my sister
   - A funny family story
   - What I have learned from my parents
   - What is most important to my family
   - A problem our family solved

3. With your partner, hold a one-minute conversation on the topic you have chosen. Use good communication skills in your conversation.

4. When it is your turn to observe a conversation, use this checklist. Check off each communication skill you observe the other two group members using in their conversation.

Speaking Skills		Listening Skills	
"I" messages		Appropriate body language	
Clear, simple statements		Conversation encouragers	
Honest thoughts and feelings		Mirror thoughts and feelings	
Appropriate body language		Ask questions	

5. After each conversation, discuss which communication skills were used.

6. Which communication skills did you use most often in your two conversations?

   Answers will vary. _____

7. Which communication skills do you need to practice?

   Answers will vary. _____

Chapter 7 Study Guide
Conflict Resolution

Chapter 7

As you read the chapter, answer the following questions. Later you can use this guide to review the information in the chapter.

Lesson 1

1. What are some different issues that can cause conflicts?

Answers will vary but may include the following points: Conflicts can be caused by

disagreements over relationships, space, property, power, rewards, and privileges.

2. What are some common places where conflicts occur, and who are these conflicts usually with?

Conflict can occur at home and can be with parents or siblings. Conflicts can occur at

school and can be with teachers or classmates. Sometime conflicts at school involve

a bully.

3. What is a bully?

A bully is someone who picks on individuals who are smaller or weaker.

4. What are conflicts with brothers and sisters usually about?

These disagreements are usually over property, space, or competition between siblings.

Sometimes brothers and sisters can take things that belong to another sibling without

asking. A younger brother or sister may cause conflict when he or she does not get the

same freedoms as an older sibling.

Chapter 7 Study Guide
Conflict Resolution

Lesson 2

5. Name some factors or emotions that fuel conflict.

Answers will vary but may include some of the following points: Factors and emotions

that fuel conflict are anger, jealousy, group pressure, and the use of alcohol or drugs.

6. What are some healthy ways to deal with anger?

Answers will vary but may include the following points: Avoid yelling. Yelling can only

create a bigger conflict. Step away from the situation. Be quiet for a few moments.

Share your feelings with a friend or trusted adult. Focus your attention on something

other than your anger and its source.

7. What are some of the negative consequences of jealousy, and what
are some healthy ways to deal with jealousy?

Answers will vary but may include the following points: Jealousy can lead to anger and

resentment, ruin a friendship, and even cause someone to seek revenge. Deal with jeal-

ousy issues by talking to a trusted adult or by writing about your feelings in a journal.

8. Why is putting yourself in someone else's situation a good way to
keep conflicts from escalating?

You might find you are better able to understand and be more sympathetic to their

viewpoint and therefore resolve the conflict with greater ease.

Lesson 3

9. What is mediation, and when should it be used?

Mediation is a process in which a third person, a mediator, helps those in conflict find a

solution. Mediation should be used when a conflict is too overwhelming or dangerous to

resolve on your own.

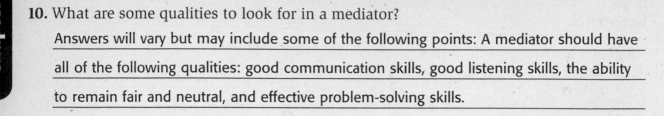

Chapter 7 Study Guide
Conflict Resolution

10. What are some qualities to look for in a mediator?

Answers will vary but may include some of the following points: A mediator should have

all of the following qualities: good communication skills, good listening skills, the ability

to remain fair and neutral, and effective problem-solving skills.

_____

11. Why is the win-win solution the best kind of solution to a conflict?

A win-win solution is an agreement or outcome that gives each party something it wants.

With this type of resolution there are no losers.

12. Why do teens make good mediators for their peers?

Answers will vary but may include some of the following points: Teens make good

mediators for their peers because they understand the attitudes and views of other

teens. They can communicate well with other teens.

_____

Activity 21
Use with Chapter 7, Lesson 1

Understanding the Causes of Conflict

Knowing the cause of a conflict often helps people find an effective way to deal with the conflict.

Read the description of conflicts in the first column. In the next column, write the reason for the conflict. In the last column, write a healthy way to deal with the conflict.

Conflict	Reason	Healthy Way to Deal With the Conflict
1. Your mom insists that you come directly home after school and complete all homework before you see your friends. You can not go out after dinner on school nights. You are angry with your mother, but do not say anything.	This is an internal conflict. You are resentful about the limits your mother has set.	It would probably help to try to see things from your mother's point of view. She has set a limit for your well-being and success in school. You need to keep a positive relationship with her.
2. Your sister's boyfriend uses your video games without asking.	This conflict involves property rights.	It would help to discuss this with your family.
3. Your teacher will not allow you to talk to your friends or write notes while he is teaching. You have had several detentions and missed track practice. Now your track coach is annoyed with you.	This is a conflict with authority.	You need to accept the teacher's authority and avoid getting detentions.
4. A group of girls makes unkind remarks about your clothes and shoes every day when you walk down the hall.	Teasing is a form of bullying by people who are seeking attention by insulting others.	You can try making jokes about your clothes yourself, but if that does not help, the bullying must be confronted by telling the girls how you feel about their remarks.
5. Several students in your chemistry class have accused you of stealing chemicals. They talk about people of your race being thieves and drug dealers.	This is bullying based on prejudice.	Do not tolerate this. Report this to the school counselor or official.
6. Every day when you sit down at the lunch table, a group of girls walks by and takes food off your tray, saying things like "You don't need any more calories!"	This is bullying by people who are trying to show they are tough by taking the property of another.	Do not tolerate this. Report this to the school counselor or official.

Activity 22

Use with Chapter 7, Lesson 2

The Truth About Preventing Conflicts

Some of the following statements about preventing conflicts are facts and others are not. Classify each statement by writing *true* or *false* in the space at the left. Correct the ones you have identified as false on the lines that follow the statements.

_____true_____ 1. A first step in preventing conflicts from turning violent is recognizing that a conflict is building.

_____

_____

_____false_____ 2. Seeking revenge always helps a jealous person get what he or she wants.

Seeking revenge never helps a jealous person get what he or she wants.

It can also escalate the conflict from a minor one to a major one.

_____false_____ 3. When a fight is developing, encouraging those involved shows good character.

When a fight occurs, encouraging those involved shows poor character.

Instead, you should show disapproval.

_____true_____ 4. Two emotions that fuel conflict are anger and jealousy.

_____

_____

_____false_____ 5. Drinking alcohol helps most people deal with conflict in a healthier way.

Typically, alcohol will make matters worse, sometimes causing the conflict to

turn violent.

_____true_____ 6. Learning to accept and appreciate people who are different from you can help prevent conflict.

_____

_____

_____true_____ 7. Mob mentality is an example of group pressure.

_____

_____

Activity 23
Use with Chapter 7, Lesson 3

Conflict Resolution and Mediation

Complete the charts below by filling in the missing steps in the conflict-resolution and mediation processes. Then, list the characteristics of good mediators and a win-win outcome in the boxes provided.

The Conflict-Resolution Process

Step 1	**T**ake a time-out, calming down 30 minutes before discussion.
Step 2	**A** Allow each person to tell his or her side without interruption.
Step 3	**L** Let each person ask questions, staying respectful and focused on the problem.
Step 4	**K** Keep brainstorming by trying different solutions that will satisfy both sides.

The Mediation Process

First	Find a private location. The only people present should be a ___mediator___ and ___the two parties with the problem___.
Second	Each party presents his or her side. The mediator stays neutral.
Sometimes	The mediator has to _ask questions to make sure each side understands_ the other's point of view.
Finally	The mediator will steer both sides toward a compromise.

Characteristics of Good Mediators

1.	Good communicators
2.	Have good listening skills
3.	Be fair and neutral judges
4.	Be effective problem solvers
5.	Be able to get to the root of the conflict

Characteristics of a Win-Win Situation

6.	An agreement that gives each party something it wants
7.	Desirable because everybody wins and nobody loses

Chapter 7

Chapter 7 Health Inventory

Conflict Prevention and Resolution

Read the statements below. In the space at the left, write *yes* if the statement describes you, or *no* if it does not describe you.

_____ **1.** I know that seeking help can prevent conflict.

_____ **2.** I respect the values of other people.

_____ **3.** When I feel my emotions running high, I step away from the situation.

_____ **4.** When I am angry, I take a moment to be quiet and feel my anger.

_____ **5.** I am able to share my feelings calmly and responsibly.

_____ **6.** I know that alcohol and other drugs can contribute to conflict.

_____ **7.** When I feel jealous of someone, I speak to a trusted adult about my feelings or write in my journal.

_____ **8.** I can accept and appreciate people who are different from me.

_____ **9.** I show respect for myself and others.

_____ **10.** I try putting myself in other people's situations.

_____ **11.** If I have a conflict with someone, I try to keep it private and not involve others.

_____ **12.** If someone has hurt me, I do not seek revenge.

_____ **13.** I try my best to get along peacefully with everyone.

_____ **14.** If someone tries to bully me, I walk away and share the matter with a trusted adult.

_____ **15.** I do not label people.

Score yourself:

Write the number of *yes* answers here. ☐

12–15: You are well informed about preventing and resolving conflicts.

8–11: You are beginning to get the message.

Fewer than 8: You still need to learn more about preventing and resolving conflicts.

Chapter 8 Study Guide
Violence Prevention

> ## Study Tips
> ✔ Read the chapter objectives.
> ✔ Look up any unfamiliar words.
> ✔ Read the questions below before you read the chapter.

As you read the chapter, answer the following questions. Later you can use this guide to review the information in the chapter.

Lesson 1

1. Define *drug trafficking*.

Drug trafficking is the buying or selling of drugs.

2. Identify three factors that influence teen violence.

Three factors that influence teen violence are (any three): gangs, the availability of

weapons, and the use of drugs.

Lesson 2

3. What are two violent crimes that often occur together?

Two violent crimes that often occur together are assault and battery.

4. How can a person avoid becoming a rape victim?

A person can avoid becoming a rape victim by staying with a group when walking or going

on dates.

5. What are two ways you can help to prevent violence?

Two ways you can help to prevent violence are reporting any crimes that you see and joining

organizations that help to educate teens about violence and help victims of violence.

Lesson 3

6. What is intimidation?

Intimidation is purposely frightening another person through threatening words, looks,

or body language.

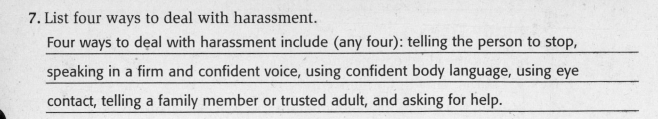

Chapter 8 Study Guide
Violence Prevention

Chapter 8

7. List four ways to deal with harassment.

Four ways to deal with harassment include (any four): telling the person to stop,

speaking in a firm and confident voice, using confident body language, using eye

contact, telling a family member or trusted adult, and asking for help.

Lesson 4

8. Define domestic violence.

Domestic violence is physical abuse that occurs within a family.

9. In the case of sexual abuse, who is usually the abuser?

In sexual abuse, an adult such as a family member or close family friend is usually

the abuser.

10. What are some of the self-destructive behaviors that victims of abuse
sometimes experience?

Victims of abuse sometimes experience self-destructive behaviors such as intentionally

hurting themselves, abusing drugs and alcohol, eating disorders, and suicide.

Lesson 5

11. How can victims break the cycle of abuse?

Victims can break the cycle of abuse by reporting the crime to a trusted adult, a crisis hot

line, or the police.

12. Where can victims of abuse go to if they feel they are in danger?

Victims of abuse can seek safety at shelters and community-run residences if they feel

they are in danger.

Activity 24
Use with Chapter 8, Lesson 1

Causes of Violence

In the chart below, list how each of the factors on the left can contribute to violence.

Factor	How The Factor Causes Violence
1. Media	Many researchers believe that teens imitate the violence that they see in the media. In the media, violence is portrayed as acceptable, influencing teens' attitudes toward violence.
2. Gangs	Members may carry guns. Members may use alcohol and drugs. Members may engage in drug trafficking. Gangs fight other gangs.
3. Availability of Weapons	A person who carries a gun is twice as likely to be injured by gun violence.
4. Drugs	A person who is under the influence of drugs is more likely to be violent because he or she cannot think clearly and does not have good judgment. Drug users commit acts of violence so they can get more drugs.

5. Make a sign with a slogan to carry at a stop-the-violence rally.
Answers will vary.

Activity 25
Use with Chapter 8, Lesson 2

Dealing With Violence

Imagine that you are a police officer who will speak at an assembly on dealing with violence. You have prepared your notes on assault and battery, rape, being attacked, and stopping violence.

Complete the note cards below.

The Way Assault and Battery Go Together:

1. Assault is a threat or attempt to do bodily injury and battery is the actual beating or hitting of another person. Often people who threaten to harm another do go on to beat the person.

The Most Common Victims Are:

2. In domestic abuse, the most common victims are women and
3. children

The Facts about Rape:

7. In 70 percent of the rape cases involving teens, the attacker and the victim know each other.

8. Rape is a crime.

9. Rape is never the victim's fault.

If attacked, the 3 Things a Person Should Do:

4. Get medical attention.

5. Report the incident to the police.

6. Get treatment for the emotional effects.

The Ways to Avoid Rape:

10. Avoid going anywhere with a date where you are all alone.

11. Do not let anyone touch you in a way that makes you feel uncomfortable.

12. Go places with groups of peers.

13. It is your right to say no and control your own body.

What You Can Do to Stop Violence:

14. Report any acts of violence that you see.

15. Become an advocate for safety and victims' rights.

Activity 26
Use with Chapter 8, Lesson 3

Harassment Hot Line

Imagine that you work for a harassment hot line. Your job is to answer questions, offer explanations, and make suggestions to the people who call.

Write an answer on the lines provided to each of the following call-in questions.

Caller # 1: In math class I sit at a table of boys. When we have group assignments, these boys will not allow me to participate. They say girls cannot solve problems. What should I do?

This is a form of gender discrimination. Tell the boys this treatment is unacceptable. If they

do not stop, talk to the teacher.

Caller # 2: Every day the same group of girls messes up my hair and touch my arms. I am a guy who likes girls, but I do not like this. Please explain.

This is sexual harassment because the touching is unwelcome. Tell the girls to stop.

Caller # 3: Yesterday, a group of rough kids walked very close to me— too close. Then, they said things like, "We'll get you later," and "Sure hope you can fight." I'm not big or strong. What should I do?

This is intimidation by bullies who probably have low self-esteem. Tell them to stop and

walk away. Then report the incident to school officials.

Caller # 4: I'm a girl. This morning in a doorway, a boy blocked my way by standing so close to me that I would have to brush against him to get out the door. Luckily, the bell rang and he ran off. What was his problem?

This is sexual harassment; it should be reported. The offender lacks respect for women.

Caller # 5: Some girls I know enjoy making fun of my pale skin. They ask questions like, "Were you born in a cave?" or "Do you live under a rock?" How should I respond?

Respond with an "I" statement. You could say, "I find your comments offensive," or

"I don't find you funny."

Activity 27
Use with Chapter 8, Lesson 4

Truths and Myths About Abuse

Read each of the following statements about abuse. If the statement is accurate, check it. If it is not accurate, correct it in the space provided.

Statements	Check	Corrections
1. Victims of abuse often blame themselves.	✔	
2. Enabling causes domestic abuse because the victim threatens the abuser with criminal charges, creating tension.		Enabling is not a cause of abuse. However, by making excuses for the abuser, the victim does establish a pattern of abuse.
3. Emotional abuse involves physical harm to a victim, so the victim feels helpless.		Emotional abuse uses words or gestures to make a person feel helpless and worthless.
4. During school, sexual abuse that includes jokes, gestures, and notes of a sexual nature should be ignored.		Sexual abuse should never be ignored; it must be reported.
5. Sometimes abusers use bribes to persuade a child to perform sexual acts.	✔	
6. In domestic abuse cases, the abuser may seek to maintain authority over the family by pushing and slapping.	✔	
7. There is no help for victims of abuse. The damage has been done and the scars remain.		Help does exist for victims of abuse.
8. Fortunately, emotional abuse is forgotten quickly.		The effect of emotional abuse is just as severe and longer lasting than bruises.
9. There are few cases of American children being neglected. Americans tend to spoil their children.		More that 2 million cases of child abuse and neglect are reported each year in America.
10. Abuse of teenagers is mainly a problem of people living in poverty.		Abuse knows no boundaries. It affects all economic groups.
11. Enabling establishes a pattern of abuse.	✔	
12. People who have been abused may develop self-destructive behaviors.	✔	

Chapter 8

Activity 28
Use with Chapter 8, Lesson 5

Help For Abuse

Complete each sentence using the words in the box.

crisis hot line	emotional trauma
cycle	help
enablers	fear
shelters	abuse
sexual	group counseling sessions

1. Whenever _____ abuse _____ is present in a family, all members are affected.

2. Some abused people are considered _____ enablers _____ because they conceal the abuse.

3. The _____ cycle _____ of abuse is a pattern of abuse that goes back generations because children who experience abuse see this behavior as a model of how to live.

4. A _____ crisis hot line _____ is a toll-free telephone service where abuse victims can get help.

5. If abuse is _____ sexual _____, people may feel ashamed and find reporting the abuse uncomfortable.

6. Victims of abuse may _____ fear _____ that telling about the abuse will lead to the break-up of their family.

7. In spite of promises to stop, the only way an abuser will ever stop is to get _____ help _____.

8. Victims of abuse need help getting over the _____ emotional trauma _____ of their abuse.

9. Sometimes abuse victims need to go to _____ shelters _____ for protection.

10. _____ Group counseling sessions _____ provide a chance for victims of abuse to discuss their situation with others who have experienced similar problems.

Applying Health Skills

Chapter 8

Practicing Healthful Behaviors

Protecting Yourself

With other students, create and perform a skit about ways to prevent violence.

Answers will vary. Possible responses provided.

1. With your partner or group, list at least five ways to prevent violence.

   Avoid drugs, gangs, and weapons. Develop a personal "zero tolerance policy" toward

   violence. Encourage others to resolve conflicts peacefully. Be a member of a neighbor-

   hood watch program. Do not walk alone at night or carry your wallet or purse where

   it is easy for someone to grab. Stay in familiar neighborhoods.

2. Plan a short skit in which the characters discuss or demonstrate ways to prevent violence. Use the ideas you have listed above. Write a brief description of the situation, the characters, and the action of your skit.

   Skits will vary, but should clearly demonstrate ways to prevent violence.

   _____

   _____

   _____

   _____

3. Together, practice acting out your skit.

4. Perform your skit for the rest of the class.

Chapter 9 Study Guide
Physical Activity and Fitness

> ### Study Tips
> ✔ Read the chapter objectives.
> ✔ Look up any unfamiliar words.
> ✔ Read the questions below before you read the chapter.

As you read the chapter, answer the following questions. Later you can use this guide to review the information in the chapter.

Lesson 1

1. Why is physical activity important?

Physical activity is important because it benefits all three sides of your health triangle.

2. Name three characteristics of people who are physically fit.

Three characteristics of people who are physically fit include (any three): having more energy; handling stress more efficiently; higher self esteem; and living longer.

3. Define *anaerobic exercise* and name two examples.

Anaerobic exercise is intense physical activity that requires little oxygen and uses short bursts of energy. Examples of anaerobic exercise are weight lifting, gymnastics, and football.

Lesson 2

4. Name three exercises that can improve your muscle strength and muscle endurance.

Three exercises that can improve your muscle strength and endurance are weight lifting, push-ups, and sit-ups.

5. What instrument is used to measure body composition?

A skinfold caliper is used to measure body composition.

Chapter 9 Study Guide
Physical Activity and Fitness

6. What are the five elements of fitness?

The five elements of fitness are heart and lung endurance, muscle endurance, muscle

strength, flexibility, and body composition.

Lesson 3

7. What is cross-training and why is it beneficial?

Cross-training is switching between different activities and exercises on different days.

Cross-training is beneficial because it allows you to do new things and to choose

activities that you will enjoy doing.

8. Why is creating a fitness schedule so important?

Creating a fitness schedule is important because you can see when you have the most

free time, consider weather and seasonal elements, balance your activities, and stay

focused on your fitness goals.

9. What does F.I.T.T. stand for?

F.I.T.T. stands for Frequency, Intensity, Time, and Type.

Lesson 4

10. Define *conditioning* and name three ways athletes can condition themselves.

Conditioning is regular physical activity and exercise that prepares a person for a sport.

Three ways athletes can condition themselves include (any three): spending many hours

practicing a sport; weight training and other exercises; maintaining a healthy diet; and

getting enough rest.

11. Why is it so important to drink plenty of water when exercising or playing a sport?

It is important to drink plenty of water when exercising or playing a sport because you

can suffer from dehydration and heat exhaustion if your body loses too much water.

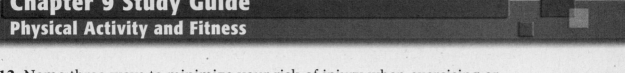

Chapter 9 Study Guide
Physical Activity and Fitness

12. Name three ways to minimize your risk of injury when exercising or playing a sport.

Three ways to minimize your risk of injury when exercising or playing a sport include: _____

using proper equipment; knowing your limits; properly taking care of your injuries. _____

_____

_____

_____

_____

_____

_____

_____

_____

_____

_____

_____

Chapter 9

Activity 29
Use with Chapter 9, Lesson 1

The Effects of Exercise

Write the specific effects of regular physical activity in each of the boxes below.

Effects

Regular Physical Activity
> **1. On Physical Health**
> Physical activity gives you more energy, helps your heart and lungs work more efficiently, strengthens your bones, improves coordination and balance, helps you sleep better, and helps you maintain a healthy weight.

Regular Physical Activity
> **2. On Social Health**
> Physical activity helps you feel comfortable in social settings. It helps you to find healthy, active things to do that will help you meet new people.

Regular Physical Activity
> **3. On Mental and Emotional Health**
> Physically active people are better able to handle the stress and challenges of everyday life. They also tend to feel better about themselves.

Physical Fitness
> **4. Provides:**
> Physically fit people have energy in reserve. They tend to live longer.

Aerobic Exercise
> **5. Benefits:**
> Aerobic exercise benefits your heart and lungs.

Anaerobic Exercise
> **6. Builds:**
> Anaerobic exercise builds muscle strength.

Activity 30
Use with Chapter 9, Lesson 2

Endurance, Strength, and Flexibility

Complete the following sentences, writing your responses on the blanks provided.

1. Doctors measure blood pressure to _know how well your heart pumps blood throughout_ your body.

2. Doctors measure heart and lung endurance to see _how efficiently your heart and lungs_ work when you exercise and how quickly they return to normal when you stop.

3. Muscle strength is _the most weight you can lift or the most force you can exert at_ one time.

4. Muscle endurance is _a muscle's ability to repeatedly exert a force over a prolonged_ period of time.

5. Weight lifting can be used to _strengthen every muscle group._

6. Swimming builds both heart and lung endurance and provides a _total body workout._

7. You can endure if you can _"last," or work and play for long periods of time without_ running out of energy.

8. Flexibility is _the ability of your body's joints to move easily through a full range_ of motion.

9. Body composition is _the ratio of body fat to lean body tissue such as bone, muscle,_ and fluid.

10. You can improve your body composition by _changing your eating habits and increasing_ your physical activity.

Chapter 9

Activity 31
Use with Chapter 9, Lesson 3

Your Fitness Plan

Create your own fitness plan by filling in the chart below.   Answers will vary.

Steps	Your Plan
Step 1: Your goals:	
Step 2: Select the activities that you will do, including: Aerobic Exercises Anaerobic Exercises Cross-Training Activity Equipment needed	
Step 3: Determine your schedule: School Physical Activities Outside Activities that involve physical activity Plan to build up your activity gradually in terms of **F**requency **I**ntensity **T**ime **T**ype	
Step 4: Monitor your heart rate: Resting heart rate: Target heart rate:	
Step 5: The warm-ups and cooldowns that you intend to use:	

Activity 32
Use with Chapter 9, Lesson 4

Sports Conditioning

Read the following descriptions related to sports conditioning. Identify the term that is being described and write the name of the term on the line provided.

Knowing Limits	Treating Injuries
Weather-Related Injuries	Proper Gear
Sports Nutrition	Minimizing Risk

___Sports Nutrition___ **1.** Eat carbohydrates like fruits, vegetables, and whole-grain products before a game or event. Avoid candy and other foods high in simple sugars.

___Sports Nutrition___ **2.** Drink plenty of water, at least 8 ounces just before a game.

___Minimizing Risk___ **3.** Progress in your activity gradually.

___Proper Gear___ **4.** Get the proper shoes and safety equipment.

___Knowing Limits___ **5.** Stop participating in the activity if you are in pain.

___Treating Injuries___ **6.** Use the PRICE formula to find relief from injury or muscle soreness.

___Weather-Related Injuries___ **7.** Prevent dehydration.

___Weather-Related Injuries___ **8.** Prevent frostbite and hypothermia.

___Minimizing Risk___ **9.** Use warm-ups and cooldowns.

Chapter 9

Chapter 9 Health Inventory

Physical Activity and Fitness

Read the statements below. In the space at the left, write *yes* if the statement describes you, or *no* if it does not describe you.

_____ **1.** I get 60 minutes of activity on most days.

_____ **2.** I am able to handle the stress and challenges of everyday life.

_____ **3.** I am comfortable in social situations.

_____ **4.** I have good endurance.

_____ **5.** I set goals to achieve a greater fitness level.

_____ **6.** I improve my flexibility by stretching, turning, and bending.

_____ **7.** I eat a well-balanced diet.

_____ **8.** I choose physical activities that I enjoy.

_____ **9.** I take advantage of the benefits of cross-training when I exercise.

_____ **10.** I always use protective gear if the activity requires it.

_____ **11.** I am practical and realistic in scheduling physical activity.

_____ **12.** I put my fitness plan in writing.

_____ **13.** I try my best to get along peacefully with everyone.

_____ **14.** I use the **F.I.T.T.** principle to avoid injury.

_____ **15.** I always warm up and cool down.

Score yourself:

Write the number of *yes* answers here.

12–15: You are well informed about physical activity and fitness, and their benefits.

8–11: You are beginning to understand about physical activity and fitness, and their benefits.

Fewer than 8: You still need to learn more about physical activity and fitness, and their benefits.

Chapter 10 Study Guide
Nutrition for Health

> ## Study Tips
> ✔ Read the chapter objectives.
> ✔ Look up any unfamiliar words.
> ✔ Read the questions below before you read the chapter.

As you read the chapter, answer the following questions. Later you can use this guide to review the information in the chapter.

Lesson 1

1. What is nutrition?

   Nutrition is the study of nutrients and how the body uses them.

2. What is the difference between appetite and hunger?

   Appetite is the psychological desire for food, whereas hunger is the body's physical

   need for food.

3. Why do many people not get enough nutrients?

   Many people do not get enough nutrients because they have poor eating habits.

Lesson 2

4. What are the health benefits of eating fiber?

   Fiber helps to push other foods through the digestive system and can lower your risk of

   some types of cancer and heart disease.

5. What are proteins made up of?

   Proteins are made up of amino acids.

6. Name three minerals that your body needs to function properly.

   Three minerals your body needs to function properly are (any three): calcium;

   phosphorus; magnesium; fluoride; iron; potassium; and zinc.

Chapter 10 Study Guide
Nutrition for Health

Lesson 3

7. What are the six sections in the MyPyramid food guidance system?

   The six sections in the MyPyramid food guidance system are grains, vegetables, fruits,

   milk, meats and beans, and fats.

8. Why is it important to balance the calories you consume with physical activity?

   Balancing calories consumed with physical activity will help you maintain a healthy

   weight.

9. What condition can an excess of sodium lead to?

   An excess of sodium can lead to high blood pressure.

Lesson 4

10. Why is breakfast such an important meal?

    Breakfast is an important meal because your body needs energy from food when you

    wake up.

11. How can you balance your eating plan? How can it help you?

    You can balance your eating plan by keeping a journal of all the foods you eat. This can

    help you better see what foods you are eating and make healthier food choices.

12. What should you look for when choosing a snack?

    When choosing a snack you should look for the nutrient density of the food.

Chapter 10

Activity 33
Use with Chapter 10, Lesson 1

Food Choices

Many factors influence what foods we eat. Among these influences are *family and friends, cultural background, food availability, time and money resources, advertising, knowledge of nutrition,* and *personal preferences.* **Read the following situations. Identify which factor or factors might have influenced the person's food choices.**

Situation 1

Bethany is on a tight budget. She purchases many of the foods she eats based on whether or not she has a coupon for it. When she can, she splurges on foods she has seen in her favorite magazine.

time and money resources; advertising

Situation 2

Sam's mother is a pediatrician. She tries to make sure that her family always eats nutritious meals.

knowledge of nutrition

Situation 3

Myrna does not have much time for breakfast. She would have rather had a bagel, but the donut shop was out of bagels. She bought a sugar donut instead.

food availability; time and money resources

Situation 4

Damien is a college student who does not have much money or time to cook. He has been eating a lot of pasta, beans, and vegetables.

knowledge of nutrition; time and money resources

Situation 5

Yoshi's family is from Japan. Her family eats many dishes with fish and vegetables. Her mother also makes sushi often.

family and friends; cultural background

Situation 6

On his way home from school every day, Dan stops at a convenience store. Instead of buying chips and soda, he always chooses a bottle of juice and a box of raisins.

time and money resources; knowledge of nutrition; personal preference

Chapter 10

Activity 34
Use with Chapter 10, Lesson 2

Letter Scramble

Unscramble the capitalized words in the sentences below. Then write the words on the lines below. On the numbered lines at the bottom of the page, write the boxed letters from the words you have unscrambled. They will form a two-word message.

1. f i b e r
2. v i t a m i n s
3. p r o t e i n s
4. c h o l e s t e r o l
5. m i n e r a l s
6. f a t s
7. b a r l e y
8. s a t u r a t e d
9. f i s h
10. c a r b o h y d r a t e s

1. REFIB is a special type of complex carbohydrate found in raw fruits, vegetables, and whole grains.

2. TIVMANIS help your body to fight infections.

3. SNIEPTOR are nutrients your body uses to build, repair, and maintain cells and tissues.

4. STRELOELOCH is a fatty substance found in the blood.

5. SLRANEMI are elements that help form healthy bones and teeth, and regulate certain body processes.

6. Saturated STAF are solid at room temperature.

7. BLEYRA is an example of a whole grain.

8. Foods like butter, cheese, and fatty meats are high in DETRAUTAS fats.

9. Amino acids are found in beef, pork, poultry, eggs, and IFHS.

10. BRACHODYATERS are sugars and starches that occur naturally in foods, mainly in plants.

E a t   h e a l t h y !

1 2 3   4 5 6 7 8 9 10

Chapter 10

Activity 35
Use with Chapter 10, Lesson 3

Knowing the Facts

Read each situation below, in which the teen described could make a healthier choice. In the space provided, write a better choice for the teen.

1. Lauren does not like vegetables. Most days her diet does not contain any foods from this food group.

   A healthy diet includes foods from all the food groups. Lauren should experiment and

   find some vegetables that she does like.

2. Adam ate breakfast and lunch at his favorite fast-food restaurant. Later, he was surprised to learn that his calorie intake for those two meals was 2,500 calories.

   Adam should limit his calories per meal so that he does not take in more calories than

   his body burns.

3. Christa was cutting vegetables for her family's dinner when she heard her dog barking from the backyard. She let the dog in, petted him, and went right back to preparing dinner.

   Christa needs to wash her hands to remove germs before preparing food.

   _____

4. Luis made himself a frozen pizza for lunch but only ate one quarter of it. He left the rest of the pizza out on the counter for his dad to eat when he got home for dinner.

   Food needs to be refrigerated to keep harmful bacteria from growing on it.

   _____

5. The only kind of chicken Danielle will eat is chicken that has been deep fried.

   Cutting down on fried foods will help limit your fat intake. Danielle should try broiled or

   grilled chicken as an alternative selection.

Chapter 10

Activity 36

Menu Planning

The key to a balanced eating plan is advanced planning. Prepare a menu plan for the next three days by completing the chart below. Use the MyPyramid illustration in your textbook for guidance.

Menu Plan

	Day 1	Day 2	Day 3
Breakfast	Answers will vary. Students should include a balanced food plan according to the MyPyramid chart.		
Lunch			
Snack			
Dinner			

Chapter 10

Applying Health Skills

Advocacy

Eating for Your Health

With a group, plan and create a cartoon that encourages teens to make healthy food choices.

1. Think about how you can use a cartoon to convince teens that they should eat a variety of foods each day. List at least three facts about nutrition from Chapter 10 to support that idea.

_____

_____

_____

_____

_____

2. With the other members of your group, discuss how you can use a cartoon to present your idea and your supporting facts. Decide whether you will create a single-panel cartoon or a comic strip. Circle your group's choice.

           Single-Panel Cartoon   Comic Strip

3. Together, write a brief description of the cartoon you are planning.

_____

_____

_____

4. Work together to draw and write the cartoon you have planned. Use construction paper and markers or crayons.

5. Share your group's cartoon with the rest of the class.

Chapter 10

Chapter 11 Study Guide
Your Body Image

Study Tips

✔ Read the chapter objectives.

✔ Look up any unfamiliar words.

✔ Read the questions below before you read the chapter.

As you read the chapter, answer the following questions. Later you can use this guide to review the information in the chapter.

Lesson 1

1. How can you boost your body image?

You can boost your body image by doing things that make you feel good about yourself,

such as spending time with friends and family, setting goals for yourself, participating in

sports and activities, and eating well-balanced meals.

2. Define *appropriate weight*.

Appropriate weight is the weight that is best for your body.

3. What factors determine your BMI?

Your gender, height, and age determine your BMI.

4. Why is the number of overweight American children and teens at an all-time high?

The number of overweight American children and teens is at an all-time high because

they have poor eating habits and do not get enough physical activity.

5. What health risks are caused by being overweight?

Being overweight can cause strain on your heart and lungs, high blood pressure, and

type 2 diabetes.

6. How many calories should a moderately active male teen eat each day?

A moderately active male teen should eat 2,220 calories each day.

Chapter 11

Chapter 11 Study Guide
Your Body Image

Lesson 2

7. What are eating disorders?

   Eating disorders are extreme and damaging eating behaviors that can lead to sickness
   and even death.

8. What is the most common eating disorder?

   The most common eating disorder is binge-eating disorder.

9. What health concerns are associated with anorexia nervosa?

   Anorexia nervosa can cause brittle bones, low blood pressure, cardiac arrest, kidney
   failure, and death.

10. What age group is anorexia nervosa most common in?

    Anorexia nervosa is most common in females between the ages of 14 and 18.

11. How do people with bulimia nervosa purge the food they have eaten?

    People with bulimia nervosa purge their food by forcing themselves to vomit or by
    taking laxatives.

12. What are two signs that someone might have bulimia nervosa?

    Two signs that someone might have bulimia nervosa are: they go to the restroom
    immediately after finishing a meal, or have swollen cheeks from vomiting.

Chapter 11

Activity 37
Use with Chapter 11, Lesson 1

Two Eating Plans

Two eating plans are described below. Read the descriptions and answer the questions that follow.

Sara's Eating Plan

Sara wants to make sure she is ready for her gymnastics season. She has decided to have a boiled egg, grapefruit juice, and whole wheat toast for breakfast. For lunch, she will eat a piece of baked chicken leftover from last night's dinner with carrot and celery sticks. Her after-school snack will be a glass of low-fat milk and an apple. At dinner, she will eat healthful portions of whatever is prepared, but she will not have butter or sour cream on her potato, and she will have fruit for dessert instead of cake or cookies.

1. Is Sara's plan likely to be successful? Why or why not?

   Yes, this eating plan is likely to be successful because Sara is eating a balanced diet of

   low-calorie foods.

2. Explain what is healthful (or not) about Sara's plan, and what, if any, changes she should make.

   It includes all the necessary nutrients and no excess fats or sugars. She's likely to be able

   to stick to it.

Jared's Eating Plan

In order to make a weight class, Jared needs to lose 10 pounds before wrestling season starts. He has read about an all-protein diet guaranteed to take off 14 pounds in 14 days. Jared eats cottage cheese for breakfast, a cheeseburger for lunch, and a steak for dinner. As the diet instructs, he drinks eight glasses of water each day. He is dropping pounds but feels tired and grumpy all the time.

3. Is Jared's plan likely to be successful? Why or why not?

   He might achieve a short-term weight loss, but at a nutritional cost. Jared's plan includes

   no grains, fruits, or vegetables. It would be difficult for him to continue eating this way.

4. Explain what is healthful (or not) about Jared's plan and what changes, if any, he should make.

   He needs to aim for a balanced eating plan by following the MyPyramid guidelines.

5. Which eating plan is healthier?

   Sara's plan is healthier because her weight-loss plan stresses nutrition and moderation.

Chapter 11

Activity 38
Use with Chapter 11, Lesson 2

Eating Disorder Fact and Fiction

Some of the statements below are facts and others are not. Classify each by writing *fact* or *fiction* in the space at the left. On the lines that follow the statements, correct the ones you have identified as fiction.

fiction   **1.** Females are the only victims of eating disorders.

The majority of people with eating disorders are females, but not all.

fiction   **2.** Eating disorders are brought on by hunger.

Eating disorders have little to do with hunger.

fact   **3.** Having an eating disorder places a person at risk for developing severe medical problems.

_____

fiction   **4.** The most common eating disorder is anorexia nervosa.

The most common eating disorder is binging, or compulsive eating.

fact   **5.** Compulsive eaters eat even when they are not hungry.

_____

fact   **6.** People with anorexia need immediate help and unless they get it, they may die.

_____

fact   **7.** People with anorexia may think they are overweight, even if they are not.

_____

fact   **8.** People with bulimia purge food they have eaten by vomiting or taking laxatives.

_____

fiction   **9.** Telling a trusted adult about a friend with an eating disorder is an act of betrayal.

People with eating disorders need professional help.

fiction   **10.** People with bulimia usually become extremely thin.

A bulimic's weight remains relatively normal.

Chapter 11

Chapter 11 Health Inventory

Body Maintenance

Read each statement below. In the space at the left, write *yes* if the statement describes you, or *no* if it does not describe you.

_____ 1. I focus on how I feel rather than how I look.

_____ 2. I drink water or fruit juice instead of a soft drink when I'm thirsty.

_____ 3. I talk to my doctor if I'm concerned about my weight.

_____ 4. I avoid fad diets.

_____ 5. I seek the support of family and friends when I'm feeling bad about my body or my weight.

_____ 6. I set realistic goals for maintaining my weight.

_____ 7. I feel good about my body.

_____ 8. I am at an appropriate weight for my age, gender, height, and body frame.

_____ 9. I avoid using food as a way to cope with depression or stress.

_____ 10. I avoid eating fast food.

_____ 11. I try to get regular physical activity every day.

_____ 12. I try to limit my fat intake each day.

_____ 13. I pay close attention to the nutrient value of the foods I eat.

_____ 14. I base my food choices on the MyPyramid food guidelines.

_____ 15. I pay attention to portion sizes when I am eating.

Score yourself:

Write the number of *yes* answers here. ☐

12–15: Excellent. You know how to manage your weight.

8–11: Good. You understand some of the issues necessary to manage your weight.

Fewer than 8: It would be a good idea to review Chapter 11 and learn more about managing your weight.

Chapter 11

Chapter 12 Study Guide
Alcohol

> ## Study Tips
> ✔ Read the chapter objectives.
> ✔ Look up any unfamiliar words.
> ✔ Read the questions below before you read the chapter.

As you read the chapter, answer the following questions. Later you can use this guide to review the information in the chapter.

Lesson 1

1. List the problems that alcohol can cause for teens.

   Alcohol can cause growth problems, learning problems, psychological problems, sleep

   problems, health problems, legal problems, and car accidents.

2. What are some of the reasons why teens drink alcohol?

   Answers will vary but may include some of the following points. Teens drink alcohol

   because of peer pressure or because they want to fit in with friends, to relieve stress

   or relax, out of curiosity or to experiment, to try to look or feel older, because they

   see people they admire drinking alcohol, because they are exposed to the images of

   alcohol in the media, or because they believe it cannot actually hurt them.

3. What are some good alternatives to drinking alcohol?

   Answers will vary but include some of the following suggestions. Some good alterna-

   tives to drinking alcohol include playing a sport, getting involved in theater or the arts,

   volunteering in the community, and joining an advocacy group.

Lesson 2

4. What is reaction time? How does alcohol use affect a person's reaction time?

   Reaction time is the body's ability to respond quickly and appropriately to situations.

   Alcohol causes delays in reaction time.

Chapter 12

Chapter 12 Study Guide
Alcohol

5. What happens when a person consumes more alcohol than his or her liver can process?

The excess alcohol stays in the person's blood and causes intoxication.

6. What is alcohol poisoning? ·

Alcohol poisoning is a dangerous condition that results when a person drinks excessive amounts of alcohol over a short period of time. This is an overdose.

Lesson 3

7. In what ways can heavy alcohol use damage the stomach?

Alcohol irritates the stomach lining and increases the amount of stomach acid. Too much acid in the stomach can cause ulcers, which are sores that cause bleeding in the stomach. Regular drinking can also cause ongoing heartburn, which is a burning feeling felt in the stomach or throat.

8. What is binge drinking?

Binge drinking is the consumption of a large quantity of alcohol in a very short period of time.

Lesson 4

9. What are the five major symptoms of alcoholism?

The five major symptoms of alcoholism are denial, craving, loss of control, tolerance, and physical dependence.

Chapter 12 Study Guide
Alcohol

10. What are the symptoms of alcohol abuse?

The symptoms of alcohol abuse include the following: failing to fulfill responsibilities

at work, school, or home; drinking in situations that are physically dangerous; having

ongoing alcohol-related legal troubles; and continuing to drink even when alcohol use

has damaged relationships.

Lesson 5

11. What is recovery?

Recovery is the process of learning to live an alcohol-free life.

12. What is the first step in an alcoholic's recovery process?

The first step in an alcoholic's recovery process is admission. This means that the person

must admit they have a problem with alcohol use and ask for help.

Activity 39
Use with Chapter 12, Lesson 1

Say "No, No, No" to Alcohol

   Resisting peer pressure can be very difficult at times. Listed below are several ways to say no to alcohol. Complete the remaining sentences by suggesting other ways to refuse alcohol.   Answers will vary. Suggested answers are provided below.

   1. "No thanks, I'm allergic to alcohol."

   2. "No thanks, I'm in training for swim team."

   3. "No thanks, I can't use the car if I drink."

   4. "No thanks, I'm a member of SADD."

   5. "No thanks, _____ I don't like the way it makes me feel. _____"

   6. "No thanks, _____ I have to study. _____"

   7. "No thanks, _____ I'd rather eat my calories than drink them. _____"

   8. "No thanks, _____ I don't want to get into trouble with my parents. _____"

   9. "No thanks, _____ I don't want to break a law; drinking is illegal at our age. _____"

   10. "No thanks, _____ I don't need to drink to have a good time. _____"

   11. "No thanks, _____ drinking alcohol makes me sick. _____"

   12. "No thanks, _____ I don't like the taste. _____"

   13. "No thanks, _____ my parents don't approve of me drinking and I respect their opinion. _____"

   14. "No thanks, _____ I want to be a good example for my younger brother. _____"

   15. "No thanks, _____ I want to stay in control. _____"

   16. "No thanks, _____ I want to keep a clear head. _____"

   17. "No thanks, _____ I don't drink. _____"

Chapter 12

Activity 40
Use with Chapter 12, Lesson 2

Alcohol Myths

Some of the statements below are facts and others are not. Classify each by writing *fact* or *myth* in the space at the left. On the lines that follow the statements, correct the ones you have identified as myths.

_____myth_____ 1. Drinking alcohol is not as dangerous as taking drugs.

Alcohol is a depressant that has a powerful effect on the body.

_____myth_____ 2. Drinking alcohol makes you more attractive.

It is not attractive to get sick, have slurred speech, or lose control.

_____myth_____ 3. The worst that drinking can do is leave you with a hangover.

Alcohol can kill you if you drink enough of it fast enough.

_____fact_____ 4. The same amount of alcohol has a greater effect on a small person than it does on a larger one.

_____

_____fact_____ 5. Alcohol generally moves into the bloodstream faster in females than males.

_____

_____fact_____ 6. Mixing alcohol with other drugs or medicines can cause death.

_____

_____myth_____ 7. Hard liquor gets you drunk faster than beer or wine.

Alcohol is alcohol, no matter what kind you drink.

_____fact_____ 8. Two to three drinks can cause a loss of coordination and judgment.

_____

_____myth_____ 9. A cold shower and cup of coffee will take away the effects of alcohol.

Nothing speeds up the breakdown of alcohol in the body.

_____fact_____ 10. One of the greatest dangers of alcohol is its unpredictability.

_____

Chapter 12

Activity 41
Use with Chapter 12, Lesson 3

Alcohol's Effects

Match the descriptions in the left column with the part of the body adversely affected by alcohol use.

___d___ **1.** Alcohol is a depressant affecting a person's emotional health.

___a___ **2.** Alcohol is not digested like other foods. It is absorbed by tissues and goes directly into the blood. It is associated with cancer here.

___c___ **3.** A life-threatening problem associated with heavy alcohol use is cirrhosis.

___b___ **4.** Alcohol increases the amount of acid, making the lining of this part of the body red and swollen.

___e___ **5.** Alcohol can cause this to become enlarged.

___d___ **6.** Alcohol can cause this to shrink.

___c___ **7.** Alcohol interferes with this doing its job, which is to remove poisons from the blood.

___d___ **8.** Alcohol can affect memory and problem-solving abilities.

a. mouth

b. stomach

c. liver

d. brain

e. heart

Answer the following questions about alcohol use. Write your answers on the lines provided.

9. Define *binge drinking* and list some of the dangers associated with it.

Binge drinking is the consumption of a large quantity of alcohol in a short time. Some

dangers of binge drinking: death due to falls, drowning, or drunk driving; pregnancy;

being a victim of violent behavior.

10. Define *inhibition* and explain alcohol's likely effect on it.

Inhibition is a conscious or unconscious restraint on behaviors or actions. Alcohol tends

to lower people's inhibitions.

Chapter 12

Activity 42
Use with Chapter 12, Lesson 4

Treating Alcoholism

People who become alcoholics develop their drinking problems over a period of time. Experts have identified four distinct stages of alcoholism.

Read the statements below. Identify the stage of alcoholism by writing 1, 2, 3, or 4 in the space to the left.

__4__ **1.** Long periods of being intoxicated all the time.

__3__ **2.** The drinker's body is strongly addicted to alcohol.

__1__ **3.** A person starts using alcohol to relax or relieve stress.

__3__ **4.** The drinker is often absent from school or work.

__2__ **5.** The drinker begins to lie or make excuses about his or her drinking.

__2__ **6.** Saying or doing hurtful things.

Answer the following questions about alcoholism. Write your answers on the lines provided.

7. What effects can alcoholism have on a family?

Alcohol abuse is a factor in family breakups, spousal abuse, and child abuse.

8. How many families in the United States are affected by alcoholism?

One in four families in the United States is affected by alcoholism.

9. What are two support groups for families coping with alcoholism?

Al-Anon helps families and friends of alcoholics; Alateen helps young people coping

with a family member or friend who is an alcoholic.

10. List the four steps of the recovery process and describe what each involves.

Admission: admitting the problem and seeking help; Detoxification: a process in which

the alcoholic's body adjusts to functioning without alcohol; Counseling: receiving

counseling on how to live without alcohol; and Recovery: taking responsibility for

one's own life.

Chapter 12

Activity 43
Use with Chapter 12, Lesson 5

Help for the Alcohol Abuser

People who are struggling with alcohol need help, and you might be able to provide some. Place a plus sign (+) in the space to the left of the statement if the suggestion is a good one that is likely to help a drinker. Place a zero (0) in the space if the suggestion is not likely to be effective.

___+___ 1. Organize an intervention.

___+___ 2. Try to include the drinker in activities that do not involve alcohol.

___0___ 3. Threaten or bribe the drinker when he or she has a relapse.

___+___ 4. Provide the drinker with the names and phone numbers of organizations that help problem drinkers.

___0___ 5. Argue with a drinker when he or she is drunk.

___+___ 6. Let the drinker know that his or her drinking concerns you.

___0___ 7. Do nothing. Allow the drinker to remain in denial about his or her problem for as long as he or she needs to.

___+___ 8. Help the drinker feel good about quitting.

___0___ 9. Emphasize the physical and psychological pain of withdrawal that the drinker will likely face.

___+___ 10. Offer to drive the drinker home when he or she is intoxicated.

Provide the following definitions on the spaces provided.

11. Define the term *recovering alcoholic*.

    A recovering alcoholic is someone who has an addiction to alcohol but chooses to live

    without using alcohol.

12. Define the term *intervention*.

    An intervention is a gathering during which family and friends get the problem drinker

    to agree to seek help.

Chapter 12

Applying Heath Skills

Decision Making

Getting Help for Someone

With a group, role-play a scene in which one or more teens decide how to help someone who may have an alcohol problem.

1. With the members of your group, think of two realistic situations in which teens must decide how to help someone who may have an alcohol problem. On separate index cards, write a brief description of each situation. These descriptions will be collected by your teacher and distributed to other groups to role-play for the class.

2. With your group, read and discuss the situation your teacher gives you. Write brief notes showing how one teen (or several teens) in that situation can use the decision-making steps to decide how to help someone who may have an alcohol problem.

State the situation. _____ Answers will vary. _____

_____

List the options. _____

_____

Weigh the possible outcomes. _____

_____

_____

Consider your values. _____

_____

Make a decision and act. _____

_____

Evaluate your decision. _____

_____

3. Keeping the decision-making steps in mind, practice role-playing the situation your group has been given. Then perform your role-play for the class.

Chapter 12

Chapter 13 Study Guide
Tobacco

Study Tips
✔ Read the chapter objectives.

✔ Look up any unfamiliar words.

✔ Read the questions below before you read the chapter.

As you read the chapter, answer the following questions. Later you can use this guide to review the information in the chapter.

Lesson 1

1. What is tar, and how can it be harmful to the body?

Tar is a thick, oily, dark liquid that forms when tobacco burns. If tar builds up in the

lungs, it can make it hard to breathe. It can cause emphysema and lung cancer.

2. What is smokeless tobacco, and what are some of the negative effects it can have on the body?

Smokeless tobacco is ground tobacco that is chewed or inhaled through the nose.

Smokeless tobacco stains your teeth and causes bad breath. It causes tooth decay

and gum disease. It can cause sores inside your mouth that can turn into cancers of

the mouth, esophagus, larynx, stomach, and pancreas.

Lesson 2

3. Name three short-term physical effects of tobacco use.

Answers may include the following: Changes take place in brain chemistry. Withdrawal

symptoms may occur as soon as 30 minutes after the last cigarette. The heart rate and

blood pressure increase. Energy is reduced because less oxygen gets to body tissues. User

has shortness of breath, reduced energy, coughing, and more phlegm. Colds and flus are

more frequent. Allergies, asthma, bronchitis, and other serious respiratory illnesses

increase. User has upset stomach, dulled taste buds, and tooth decay.

Chapter 13 Study Guide
Tobacco

4. What is cardiovascular disease?

Cardiovascular disease is a disease of the heart and blood vessels.

Lesson 3

5. What is a psychological dependence?

A psychological dependence is an addiction in which the mind sends the body a

message that it needs more of a drug.

6. What are some of the psychological symptoms of nicotine withdrawal?

The psychological symptoms of nicotine withdrawal include irritability, sudden cravings,

difficulty concentrating, and difficulty sleeping.

Lesson 4

7. What is the difference between sidestream smoke and mainstream smoke?

Sidestream smoke is smoke that comes directly from a burning cigarette, pipe, or cigar.

Mainstream smoke is smoke that is exhaled by a smoker.

8. What is a passive smoker?

A passive smoker is a nonsmoker who breathes in secondhand smoke.

Lesson 5

9. What are point-of-sale promotions?

Point-of-sale promotions are advertising campaigns in which a product is promoted at a

store's checkout counter.

10. What are some ways you can stand up to negative peer pressure and
avoid using tobacco products?

Answers may include some of the following points: Stay away from people who use

tobacco products. You will not feel pressure from peers who do not smoke. Avoid

situations where tobacco products may be used. Use your "S.T.O.P." refusal skills:

Say no. **T**ell why. **O**ffer another idea. **P**romptly leave.

Activity 44

Use with Chapter 13, Lesson 1

Tobacco Products

Match each of the words or terms on the left with its description on the right. Write the description in the space provided.

Bidis

Carbon monoxide

Addictive

Kreteks

Tobacco

Smokeless tobacco

Nicotine

Tar

_____Bidis_____

_____Tobacco_____

_____Carbon monoxide_____

_____Tar_____

_____Addictive_____

_____Smokeless tobacco_____

_____Keteks_____

_____Nicotine_____

1. Cigarettes containing sweet, candy-like flavorings

2. A woody, shrub-like plant with large leaves

3. A poisonous, colorless, odorless gas

4. A thick, oily, dark liquid that forms when tobacco burns

5. Causing intense cravings

6. Ground tobacco that is chewed or inhaled through the nose

7. Cigarettes that contain a mixture of tobacco, cloves, and other additives

8. An addictive drug found in all tobacco products

9. What are the unhealthy effects of using smokeless tobacco?

   The unhealthy effects of using smokeless tobacco are: it contains 15 times more nicotine

   than cigarettes. It stains the teeth, causes bad breath, tooth decay, and gum disease.

   It also causes sores inside the mouth that can become cancerous.

10. Imagine you have a friend who tells you that cigar smoking is not as dangerous as cigarette smoking because you do not inhale it into your lungs. What is your response?

    You could tell your friend that smoke from the burning tobacco is released into the air

    around the smoker and inhaled. Cigar smoking contains the same addictive risk. Cigar

    smoking is linked to cancer of the mouth and throat.

Activity 45
Use with Chapter 13, Lesson 2

Tobacco's Short-Term and Long-Term Effects

In the following statements, write whether the effect is a *short-term* or *long-term* effect of using tobacco. Fill in the blanks with terms from your textbook to complete the statements.

____short-term____ 1. Tobacco use causes chemical changes to the ____brain____.

____long-term____ 2. Smoking is the leading cause of ____lung____ cancer.

____short-term____ 3. Tobacco stains the teeth and gums and increases the risk of gum ____disease____.

____long-term____ 4. Smoking causes a dry, hacking ____cough____, which is a symptom of ____COPD____.

____long-term____ 5. Smoking is a leading cause of cardiovascular disease, a disease of the ____heart____ and ____blood vessels____.

____short-term____ 6. Smoking dulls the ____taste buds____.

____short-term____ 7. Smoking increases ____respiratory illnesses____, such as asthma, allergies, and bronchitis.

____short-term____ 8. Smoking increases the user's ____heart rate____ and blood ____pressure____.

____long-term____ 9. Smoking causes ____cancer____ of the bladder.

____long-term____ 10. Smoking causes increased cholesterol ____levels____.

Activity 46
Use with Chapter 13, Lesson 3

Questions About Tobacco Use

Answer the following questions about tobacco addiction.

1. What is the best way to keep from having a tobacco-related disease?

   The best way to avoid a tobacco-related disease is never to start using tobacco.
   _____

2. What kind of drug is nicotine?

   Nicotine is a stimulant.

3. What effect does this type of drug have on the body?

   Stimulants speed up body functions, such as heart and breathing rates.

4. What are the warning signs that some people commonly experience when first using tobacco?

   Warning signs include light-headedness, nausea, and vomiting.

5. What happens once tolerance to tobacco occurs?

   The brain undergoes actual physical changes. It develops a new supply of receptors,

   structures that help the body identify and respond to sensations.

6. What is the difference between a physical dependence and a psycho-logical dependence on nicotine?

   A physical dependence is a type of addiction in which the body itself feels a direct need

   for a drug, while a psychological dependence is an addiction in which the mind sends

   the body a message that it needs more of the drug.

7. Once psychological and physical dependencies are established, what is the tobacco user considered?

   Once psychological and physical dependencies have been established, the tobacco user

   is considered an addict.

Activity 47
Use with Chapter 13, Lesson 4

Tobacco's Costs

Match the information from the column on the right with the information on the left to form a correct statement about the costs of tobacco to society. Write the letter in the space provided.

__b__ 1. For every dollar spent to spread the word about the dangers of smoking, tobacco companies spend _____ on marketing.

__e__ 2. The typical smoker spends _____ per day on tobacco.

__a__ 3. The average price per pack of cigarettes is up to _____.

__f__ 4. The average smoker spends about _____ per month on tobacco products.

__g__ 5. Each year tobacco companies spend _____ billion on advertising.

__d__ 6. America's tobacco habit costs the nation nearly _____ billion a year.

__h__ 7. Each year, the U.S. economy loses _____ billion in productivity due to smoking.

__c__ 8. In 10 years' time, the average smoker will have spent _____ thousand on tobacco.

a. $5

b. $23

c. $27

d. $240

e. $7.50

f. $225

g. $12.7

h. $80

Activity 48

Use With Chapter 13, Lesson 5

Your Anti-Smoking Campaign

Imagine that you have been asked to design several bumper stickers that will inform others on the rights of the nonsmoker. Use as few words as possible to make your points.

Answers will vary.

Chapter 13 Health Inventory

The Truth About Tobacco

Some of these statements about tobacco are true and some are false. Identify each statement by writing *true* or *false* in the space at the left.

____true____   **1.** The best way to remain tobacco-free is never to start using tobacco products.

____false____   **2.** Tobacco use has no effect on pubic health costs to the U.S. economy.

____false____   **3.** Tobacco use is not psychologically addictive.

____true____   **4.** Nonsmokers can be seriously harmed by secondhand smoke.

____false____   **5.** Cigar and pipe smokers do not run the risk of becoming addicted to nicotine.

____false____   **6.** Most smokers do not want to quit the habit.

____true____   **7.** Women who smoke during pregnancy risk premature delivery or having a low-birth-weight baby.

____true____   **8.** Several national associations sponsor programs that are designed to help people kick the tobacco habit.

____false____   **9.** Tobacco companies spend very little money on advertising, since the product "sells itself."

____false____   **10.** A small percentage of people who decide to quit smoking suffer a relapse within the first three months after quitting.

____true____   **11.** You have the right to breathe air that is free of tobacco smoke.

____true____   **12.** When tobacco smoke is inhaled, tar deposits form on the linings of the lungs.

Score yourself:

Write the number of correct responses here:

10–12: Excellent

6–9: Fair

0–5: Reread Chapter 13 to learn the facts about tobacco use.

Chapter 14 Study Guide
Drugs

Study Tips

✔ Read the chapter objectives.

✔ Look up any unfamiliar words.

✔ Read the questions below before you read the chapter.

As you read the chapter, answer the following questions. Later you can use this guide to review the information in the chapter.

Lesson 1

1. What is the difference between prescription and over-the-counter medicines?

   Prescription medicines are medicines that can be sold only with a written order from a physician. Doctors or pharmacists give specific directions on its use. Over-the-counter medicines are medicines that are safe enough to be taken without a written order from a physician. They are sold in pharmacies and stores.

2. What is the difference between drug misuse and drug abuse?

   Drug misuse is taking or using medicine in a way that is not intended. Using the drug without following the instructions, allowing someone to use a drug prescribed to you, taking more of the drug than the doctor prescribed, and using the drug longer than advised are all examples of misusing drugs. Drug abuse is intentionally using drugs in a way that is unhealthy or illegal. Both using illegal drugs and using legal drugs for nonmedical reasons are examples of drug abuse. People who abuse drugs are at risk of developing an addiction.

Lesson 2

3. What are three short-term effects of marijuana use?

   Short-term effects of marijuana use include memory and learning problems, distorted perception, and difficulty thinking and solving problems.

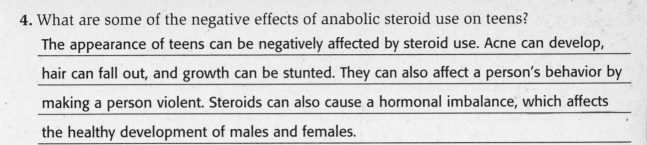

4. What are some of the negative effects of anabolic steroid use on teens?

The appearance of teens can be negatively affected by steroid use. Acne can develop,

hair can fall out, and growth can be stunted. They can also affect a person's behavior by

making a person violent. Steroids can also cause a hormonal imbalance, which affects

the healthy development of males and females.

Lesson 3

5. Name two narcotics that are commonly abused.

Two narcotics commonly abused include heroin and OxyContin. Heroin is illegal and

is most often inhaled or injected intravenously, although sometimes it is smoked.

OxyContin is legal with a doctor's prescription. It is used correctly for controlling severe

pain in cancer patients and those with arthritis.

6. Name five of the most harmful effects of stimulant abuse.

Five of the most harmful effects of stimulant abuse include: seizures, stroke, damage to

heart and nervous system, heart attacks, and death.

Lesson 4

7. Name two harmful effects of hallucinogens.

Two harmful effects of hallucinogens include flashbacks and violent or unpredictable

behavior.

8. What damage do inhalants cause a user?

Abusing inhalants can damage the coating that surrounds brain cells called myelin.

When the myelin is damaged, the nerve cells cannot send signals to the other parts of

the body. This can affect a person's ability to walk, talk, or think. Inhalants can also kill a

user instantly.

Chapter 14 Study Guide
Drugs

Lesson 5

9. What is the first step in getting help for drug abuse?

The first step in getting help for drug abuse is for the user to admit that there is

a problem.

10. Name five treatment options for individuals needing help recovering from substance abuse.

Five treatment options for individuals needing help recovering from substance abuse

include: inpatient treatment, residential programs, partial hospitalization or day

treatment, outpatient programs, and intensive outpatient treatment programs.

Lesson 6

11. What is the S.T.O.P. strategy for refusing drugs?

S.T.O.P. stands for: **S**ay no in a firm voice; **T**ell why not; **O**ffer alternative ideas or

activities; **P**romptly leave.

12. What are six healthy alternatives to drug use?

Six healthy alternatives to drug use are: begin a regular physical activity routine; volunteer

to help someone in your school or community; join a school club; take part in a drug-

free event; write down your thoughts or express them through art; balance physical

activity with rest; form friendships with people who are drug free.

Activity 49
Use with Chapter 14, Lesson 1

The Truth About Drug Abuse

Some of the statements below are facts and others are not. Classify each by writing *true* or *false* in the space at the left. On the lines that follow the statements, correct the ones you have identified as false.

_____true_____ 1. Drug addiction is a disease.

_____

_____false_____ 2. Taking more of a drug than a doctor prescribes is abuse.

It is misuse.
_____

_____false_____ 3. Side effects will not happen if you take medicines properly.

Some side effects are common, even if medicines are taken properly.
_____

_____true_____ 4. A drug tolerance might develop if you take a medicine for a long period of time.

_____

_____true_____ 5. Using legal drugs for nonmedical reasons is drug abuse.

_____

_____true_____ 6. Abusers often have trouble functioning without drugs.

_____

_____false_____ 7. Combining over-the-counter medicines is perfectly safe.

Combining over-the-counter medicines can cause harmful side effects.
_____

_____false_____ 8. To safely dispose of outdated or unused pills, simply throw them away.

Flush them down the toilet.
_____

_____true_____ 9. Drug abuse can affect all three sides of your health triangle.

_____

_____false_____ 10. An addiction means someone has a physical need for a drug.

Psychological need also implies addiction.
_____

Activity 50
Use with Chapter 14, Lesson 2

Chapter 14

Truth About Illegal Drugs

Some of the following statements about illegal drugs are facts and others are not. Classify each statement by writing *true* or *false* in the space at the left. On the lines that follow the statements, correct the ones you have identified as false.

_____true_____ 1. Marijuana users are at risks for the same lung diseases that tobacco users face, including cancer.

_____

_____

_____false_____ 2. There are approximately 100 chemicals in marijuana.

There are actually over 400 chemicals in the marijuana plant.

_____

_____false_____ 3. Amnesia is the main active chemical in marijuana.

THC is the main active chemical in marijuana. Amnesia is partial or total loss

of memory. It is one of the harmful effects of club drugs.

_____false_____ 4. People react the same way to club drugs.

All people react differently to club drugs. No one can predict what their

reaction will be.

_____false_____ 5. Ecstasy, like marijuana, comes from a plant.

Ecstasy, also known as MDMA, is a synthetic chemical, created in illegal labora-

tories. Makers of the drug often add other substances to ecstasy.

_____true_____ 6. GHB and Rohypnol have both been linked to sexual assault.

_____

_____

_____true_____ 7. Steroid use can cause a hormonal imbalance in teen users.

_____

_____

Activity 51
Use with Chapter 14, Lesson 3

Matching

Match the definitions in the left column with the appropriate term.
Write the letter in the space provided.

___b___ **1.** A drug that stimulates the central nervous system

___g___ **2.** When a drug is taken repeatedly at increasingly
high doses

___e___ **3.** Liquid from the poppy plant containing substances
that numb the body

___d___ **4.** Illegal stimulant derived from the coca plant

___a___ **5.** A feeling of well-being or elation

___f___ **6.** Used to treat patients with more serious anxiety
and panic attacks

___h___ **7.** Drugs that speed up activity in the human brain
and spinal cord

___c___ **8.** Substances that slow down normal brain function

a. Euphoria

b. Amphetamine

c. CNS depressants

d. Cocaine

e. Opium

f. Benzodiazepines

g. Binge

h. Stimulants

Answer the following questions about drugs. Write your answers on
the lines provided.

9. How do narcotics work?

Narcotics attach themselves to certain receptors in the brain to block any painful

messages that are being sent. These drugs can produce a sense of euphoria because

they affect the areas of the brain that perceive pleasure.

10. What are the harmful effects of depressants?

Harmful effects of depressants include: anxiety; reduced coordination and attention

span; mood changes and excessive sleep. High doses can cause internal bleeding,

coma, and death.

Activity 52
Use with Chapter 14, Lesson 4

Chapter 14

Understanding Hallucinogens and Inhalants

In the space, write the word from the list that will best complete each statement.

1. _____LSD_____ is a drug made from lysergic acid.

2. A(n) _____inhalant_____ is any substance whose fumes are sniffed and inhaled to produce mind-altering sensations.

3. The _____psychological_____ effects of LSD are often very difficult to predict.

4. _____PCP_____ is not a true hallucinogen in its chemical makeup, but its effects are similar to the effects of other hallucinogens.

5. _____Hallucinogens_____ are drugs that distort moods, thoughts, and senses.

6. If _____myelin_____ is damaged, nerve cells may not be able to send messages to other parts of the body.

PCP
myelin
LSD
hallucinogens
inhalant
psychological

Answer the following questions about drug use. Write your answers on the lines provided.

7. What are some of the harmful effects of hallucinogens?

Some of the harmful effects of hallucinogens include: increased blood pressure, heart

rate, and temperature; chills, nausea, tremors, and sleeplessness; unpredictable behavior.

8. What are some of the warning signs of inhalant abuse?

Some of the warning signs of inhalant abuse include: eyes that are red and runny; sores

near the mouth; breath that smells like chemicals; holding a marker near the nose.

9. What are some of the harmful effects of inhalants?

Inhalants produce a high that resembles alcohol intoxication. If sufficient amounts are

inhaled, solvents and gases produce anesthesia, loss of sensation, and unconsciousness.

10. What damage do inhalants cause?

Using inhalants can damage the protective coating that surrounds brain cells, called

myelin. As a result, nerve cells cannot send messages to other parts of the body.

Activity 53

Recognizing the Symptoms

Drug addiction is treatable. The first step to getting help is admitting that a drug problem exists. Recognizing the symptoms is key. Place a plus sign (+) in the space to the left of the statement if it describes a symptom of a person likely using drugs. Place a zero (0) in the space if the statement is not necessarily a sign of drug abuse.

__+__ 1. Dwayne always loved everything to do with baseball, including playing it, watching it, and collecting memorabilia. Yet, these days, his brother cannot convince him to even play catch.

__0__ 2. Megan's grade in algebra dropped from an A to a C in one marking period.

__+__ 3. Caitlyn's longtime friend confronts her to ask if she has a drug problem; Caitlyn laughs and denies it.

__+__ 4. Jacob realizes he needs increasingly larger amounts of drugs to get high.

__0__ 5. Jasmine is slowly losing weight.

__0__ 6. Kirsten has dyed her hair black and begun dressing all in black.

__+__ 7. Mike craves marijuana whenever his stepfather confronts him about grades.

__+__ 8. Peter is bulking up bigger and faster than anyone else on the football team.

__+__ 9. Sophie finds herself taking more drugs than she meant to, and using drugs at times and places she had not planned.

__+__ 10. Will's mom notices that money and jewelry have begun to go missing since Will started hanging out with a new group of friends.

Provide the following definitions on the spaces provided.

11. Describe *tolerance*.

Tolerance is when a person needs increasingly larger amounts of drugs to get high.

12. Describe *withdrawal symptoms*.

Withdrawal symptoms may include nausea, sweating, shaking, and extreme anxiety.

Chapter 14

Activity 54
Use with Chapter 14, Lesson 6

Say No to Drugs

Refusing to give in to peer pressure can be hard at times. Listed below are several ways to say no to drugs. Complete the remaining sentences by suggesting other ways to refuse drugs.

1. "No thanks, drugs are illegal."

2. "No thanks, I'm getting in shape."

3. "No thanks, I don't like to be out of control."

4. "No thanks, I have schoolwork to do. "

5. "No thanks, my parents don't approve and I respect their opinion. "

6. "No thanks, I'd rather stay out of trouble with the law. "

7. "No thanks, I want to keep my head clear. "

8. "No thanks, I have other plans with friends. "

9. "No thanks, I don't need to do drugs to feel cool. "

10. "No thanks, drugs are unpredictable and dangerous. "

11. "No thanks, I don't want to risk my life to fit in. "

12. "No thanks, I have goals I am working to reach. "

13. "No thanks, I have a big test coming up. "

14. "No thanks, I find other ways to feel good. "

15. "No thanks, my friends and I are not into drugs. "

16. "No thanks, I want to keep my focus on school. "

17. "No thanks, I might get hurt. "

18. "No thanks, I have heard about the side effects and dangers. "

19. "No thanks, I don't have time to waste on drugs. "

20. "No thanks!"

Applying Health Skills

Analyzing Influences

Staying Drug Free

Think of the factors that have influenced you to be drug free. Create a jigsaw puzzle showing the factors.

1. Think about the factors that have influenced you to be drug free. List the five most important factors here.

   Answer will vary. _____

   _____

   _____

   _____

   _____

2. Choose an object that symbolizes one aspect of your personality. For example, if you enjoy art, you might choose an easel or a paint brush. Name the object you have chosen.

   Objects will vary. _____

3. On a sheet of light-colored construction paper, make a large outline drawing of the object you have chosen.

4. Cut out the object you have drawn. Then cut the object into five pieces to create a jigsaw puzzle. On each puzzle piece, write one of the factors you have listed above.

5. Switch puzzles with a classmate. Put your classmate's puzzle together, and glue the pieces onto a piece of poster board.

6. Display your completed puzzle in the classroom. Look at your classmates' completed puzzles. Use tally marks to record how many other students recorded the same important factors you listed.

Chapter 15 Study Guide
Personal Care and Consumer Choices

Study Tips

✔ Read the chapter objectives.

✔ Look up any unfamiliar words.

✔ Read the questions below before you read the chapter.

As you read the chapter, answer the following questions. Later you can use this guide to review the information in the chapter.

Lesson 1

1. List the skin's basic functions.

The skin acts as a barrier against water; it protects you from germs; it helps control body

temperature; and it allows you to feel texture and alerts you of temperature.

2. Name three causes for skin problems.

Clogged oil glands can cause acne. Too much sun exposure can cause wrinkles and aging.

Viruses can cause skin problems.

3. Describe the parts of good tooth and gum care.

You should floss and gently brush the teeth to remove plaque. You should follow good

eating habits, including foods rich in calcium. You should avoid sugary foods and see a

dentist twice a year.

Lesson 2

4. What is a consumer?

A consumer is anyone who uses products or services.

5. Identify four factors that can influence a person's buying decisions.

Internal factors may include: personal taste and personal need. External factors may

include: family, cost, advertising, media messages, peers, and salespeople.

Chapter 15 Study Guide
Personal Care and Consumer Choices

Lesson 3

6. How do prescription medicines differ from nonprescription medicines?

Prescription medicines can be sold only with a written order from a physician or nurse

practitioner. Nonprescription medicines, or over-the-counter medicines, are safe enough

to be taken without a written order from a physician.

7. Define *side effect*.

A side effect is any effect other than the one intended.

8. Name three risks of medicines.

When used over a long period, some medicines can lead to tolerance. Overuse is another

risk of taking medicines. Combining medicines can be another problem. The effects of

taking two or more medicines at once can be dangerous.

Lesson 4

9. Name three types of health care facilities available in most communities.

Answers may include: surgery centers, hospice care, assisted living communities, doctors'

offices, or clinics.

10. What is managed care?

Managed care is an arrangement that saves money by limiting the choice of doctors to

patients who are members.

Lesson 5

11. Name two health programs that are overseen by the Department of Health and Human Services.

Answers may include that the Department of Health and Human Services oversees

programs in research, disease prevention, food and drug safety, abuse prevention,

and the Medicare and Medicaid systems.

Chapter 15 Study Guide
Personal Care and Consumer Choices

12. What is the job of the Consumer Product Safety Commission?

The Consumer Product Safety Commission (CPSC) works to reduce risks from unsafe

products. The CPSC will issue a recall if a product is found to cause health problems

or injury.

_____

13. What international organizations have made world health a priority?

Answers include the World Health Organization and Doctors Without Borders.

_____

Activity 55

Use with Chapter 15, Lesson 1

Skin, Teeth, Hair, and Nails

Imagine that you are on a quiz show and one of the categories is Personal Health Care. The quiz show host presents only the answers. You must supply the questions.

1. **Answer:** A physician who specializes in skin problems.

   Question: What is a dermatologist?

2. **Answer:** The outermost layer of skin.

   Question: What is the epidermis?

3. **Answer:** A hole caused by an acid formed from sugar and plaque.

   Question: What is a cavity?

4. **Answer:** The body's largest organ.

   Question: What is skin?

5. **Answer:** A soft, colorless sticky film containing bacteria that coats your teeth.

   Question: What is plaque?

6. **Answer:** The eye's clear protective structure that lets light in.

   Question: What is a cornea?

7. **Answer:** A measure of the loudness of sound.

   Question: What is a decibel?

8. **Answer:** The tough substance composing hair and nails.

   Question: What is keratin?

9. **Answer:** Hearing loss.

   Question: What is the most common hearing problem?

10. **Answer:** The thin layer of nerve cells that covers the interior back of the eye and absorbs light.

    Question: What is the retina?

Activity 56
Use with Chapter 15, Lesson 2

Becoming a Skilled Consumer

Design package labels that appeal to teens for the variety of products below. Make sure to include all important product information that smart consumers might look for. Refer to package labels at home and at stores for ideas about ingredients, etc.

Toothpaste   Answers will vary. Sample responses provided.

Product name: Whiter Than That! _____

Amount in container: 4 oz. _____

Product's intended use: Comprehensive dental care with emphasis on whitening _____

Warnings: May cause super sensitivity to hot and cold for a short time after use. _____

Directions for use: Put a small amount on toothbrush, and brush for 2 minutes twice daily.

Ingredients: Fluoride, Baking Soda, Mint Flavoring _____

Manufacturer's contact information: Call 1-800-Whitest for customer service. _____

Acne cream

Product name: _____

Amount in container: _____

Product's intended use: _____

Warnings: _____

Directions for use: _____

Ingredients: _____

Manufacturer's contact information: _____

Shampoo

Product name: _____

Amount in container: _____

Product's intended use: _____

Warnings: _____

Directions for use: _____

Ingredients: _____

Manufacturer's contact information: _____

Activity 57
Use with Chapter 15, Lesson 3

Take Your Medicine—Wisely!

Read each situation. Then answer the questions below.

Situation 1
Jessica's grandmother has a heart condition and lives in an assisted living facility with many other senior citizens. As winter approaches, the doctor urges her to protect herself against the flu. What type of medicine is used to prevent flu?

A vaccine is used to prevent flu.

Situation 2
Molly has a toothache. The dentist has no appointments open until tomorrow. What type of medicine might help Molly?

An over-the-counter pain killer such as aspirin or ibuprofen might help Molly.

Situation 3
Jared has a sore throat, and his doctor diagnosed it as strep. What medicine will help Jared?

A prescription antibiotic will help Jared.

Situation 4
Sara took a pill this morning for her hay fever and it relieved her stuffy nose and itchy eyes, but by the time she's reached her first-period class, she feels very sleepy. Why?

Drowsiness is one of the common side effects listed on the package of pills.

Situation 5
Matt's baby brother has a doctor's appointment and the doctor gives him a shot even though the infant is healthy and happy. What kind of medicine did the doctor administer and why?

The doctor gave the baby a vaccine to prevent against childhood diseases such as measles,

mumps, chicken pox, etc.

Situation 6
Cara twists her ankle during cheerleading practice. In addition to getting rest, Cara might consider taking what kind of medicine?

Cara should take an over-the-counter painkiller/anti-inflammatory such as ibuprofen.

Activity 58
Use with Chapter 15, Lesson 4

Chapter 15

Choosing a Specialist

Read each statement below. Then decide which health care specialist would be the best one to visit for treatment. Write the letter of the appropriate provider in the space at the left.

___c___ 1. When B.J. had a physical before trying out for the football team, his doctor told him he had a heart murmur and advised him to see this specialist.

___b___ 2. Jen's younger brother, who has leukemia, is under the care of this specialist.

___d___ 3. Nadine has been sad for more than a month. She has lost interest in the activities she used to love and her grades are dropping. She feels hopeless.

___e___ 4. Bryan wants to make the wrestling team and compete in a weight class that requires him to gain 10 pounds. His brother told him to eat lots of French fries and chocolate bars, but his father made him an appointment with this specialist.

___b___ 5. Lisette's aunt, who has been diagnosed with breast cancer, is undergoing chemotherapy when she visits this specialist.

___c___ 6. Ian's grandfather needs his pacemaker checked regularly by this specialist.

___d___ 7. This specialist might find him or herself testifying in court about the sanity of an accused criminal.

___f___ 8. Kelly suffers from severe headaches, so her mother made an appointment for her to see this specialist.

a. osteopath

b. oncologist

c. cardiologist

d. psychiatrist

e. dietitian

f. neurologist

Activity 59
Use with Chapter 15, Lesson 5

Public Health

Some of the statements below are true and others are not. Classify each by writing *true* or *false* in the space at the left. On the lines that follow the statements, correct the ones you have identified as false.

___true___   **1.** Every county in every state has its own public health department.

_____

___false___   **2.** At the federal level, public health is overseen by the National Institutes of Health.

It is overseen by the Department of Health and Human Services.

___false___   **3.** An announcement that informs the public that a product has been determined unsafe is a public service announcement.

This announcement is a recall.

___true___   **4.** The Consumer Product Safety Commission works to reduce risks from unsafe products.

_____

___true___   **5.** The Department of Health and Human Services is responsible for the Medicare and Medicaid systems.

_____

___false___   **6.** The American Cancer Society is the world's premier medical research organization.

The National Institutes of Health is the premier medical research organization.

___true___   **7.** In many places around the globe, populations are faced with famine.

_____

___true___   **8.** The World Health Organization is an agency of the United Nations.

_____

___true___   **9.** The Indian Health Service is one of the main agencies of the Department of Health and Human Services.

_____

___false___   **10.** The American Heart Association is paid for by tax dollars.

This organization exists purely through donations of money and time.

Chapter 15 Health Inventory

Personal Care

Read the questions below. In the space at the left, write *yes* **if the item describes you, or** *no* **if it does not describe you.**

_____ **1.** I know my rights as a consumer.

_____ **2.** I compare products before I buy.

_____ **3.** I care about getting the best product for my money.

_____ **4.** I know where to get help for a consumer problem.

_____ **5.** I avoid being talked into purchases by salespeople.

_____ **6.** I am aware of external factors that can play a role in decision making.

_____ **7.** I look for products that offer a warranty.

_____ **8.** I keep receipts for products I have purchased.

_____ **9.** I know how to return an unsatisfactory or defective product.

_____ **10.** I have excellent consumer skills.

_____ **11.** I am able to analyze the influences on my buying practices.

_____ **12.** I have a good sense of my own personal taste.

_____ **13.** I am able to analyze advertisements on television.

_____ **14.** I read label ingredients before I buy a product.

_____ **15.** I know what to do in case of fraud.

Score yourself:

Write the number of *yes* answers here.

12–15: You are an alert consumer.

8–11: You're a fair consumer.

Fewer than 8: Buyers beware! Remember, it's your money and your health. Learn the facts.

Chapter 16 Study Guide
Your Body Systems

Study Tips

✔ Read the chapter objectives.

✔ Look up any unfamiliar words.

✔ Read the questions below before you read the chapter.

As you read the chapter, answer the following questions. Later you can use this guide to review the information in the chapter.

Lesson 1

1. How many bones are in the body?

There are 206 bones in the human body.

2. Define the three types of connective tissue.

Cartilage is a strong, flexible, gel-like tissue that cushions your joints. It reduces friction

in movement. Tendons are tough bands of tissue that attach your muscles to bones.

Ligaments are cord-like tissues that connect the bones in each joint. They hold your

bones in place.

Lesson 2

3. What are cardiac muscles?

Cardiac muscles are muscles found only in the walls of your heart. They are also

involuntary. They are at work even when you are asleep.

Lesson 3

4. What are the parts of blood?

Blood is made up of plasma, red blood cells, white blood cells, and platelets.

Chapter 16 Study Guide
Your Body Systems

5. What are capillaries?

Capillaries are tiny blood vessels that connect the veins and arteries to the body's cells.

Lesson 4

6. What are the two parts to respiration?

External respiration is the exchange of oxygen and carbon dioxide between the blood

and the air in the lungs. You breathe in oxygen to the lungs. The oxygen goes from the

lungs to the blood. Carbon dioxide goes from the blood to the lungs. Internal respiration

is cell respiration. This is the exchange of oxygen and carbon dioxide between the blood

and the cells.

7. What are some things you can do to help care for your respiratory system?

Answers may include the following: Stay active. Avoid smoking. Avoid polluted air. Avoid

outdoor activities on days with bad air quality. Reduce your risk of respiratory infection. If

someone around you is sick, be sure to wash your hands often with soap and water. Try

not to touch your nose and mouth.

Lesson 5

8. What are the two main parts of the nervous system, and what do they include?

The two main parts of the nervous system are the central nervous system and the

peripheral nervous system. The CNS includes the brain and spinal cord. The PNS includes

nerves that get information from all parts of the body and the body's environment.

Chapter 16 Study Guide
Your Body Systems

9. What are the two parts of the peripheral nervous system? Define them.

The two parts of the peripheral nervous system are the somatic system and the

autonomic system. The somatic system is a system dealing with actions that you

control. The autonomic system is a system dealing with actions you do not control.

Lesson 6

10. What is digestion?

Digestion is the process of changing food into material the body can use.

Lesson 7

11. What is the pituitary gland?

The pituitary gland is a gland that signals other endocrine glands to produce hormones

when needed.

Lesson 8

12. What is menstruation, how long does it usually last, and how often does it usually occur?

Menstruation is when the lining material, the unfertilized egg, and some blood flow out

of the body. This is also called a period. Menstruation can last 5 to 7 days and occurs

about every 28 days.

Chapter 16

Activity 60
Use with Chapter 16, Lesson 1

Your Skeletal System

From the box on the right, choose the type of joint found in the parts of the body listed on the left. Terms may be used more than once. Then identify each type of skeletal system problem described at the bottom, using the terms listed in the box.

_____Hinge_____ 1. Knees

_____Gliding_____ 2. Collar Bone

_____Ball-and-socket_____ 3. Shoulders

_____Pivot_____ 4. Between the Neck and the Head

_____Hinge_____ 5. Elbows

_____Ball-and-socket_____ 6. Hips

_____Gliding_____ 7. Ankles

Ball-and-socket
Gliding
Hinge
Pivot

_____Scoliosis_____ 8. A disorder in which the spine curves to one side of the body

_____Osteoporosis_____ 9. A bone disorder most often seen in older adults in which the bones become brittle

_____Dislocation_____ 10. Occurs when a bone is pushed out of its joint

_____Fracture_____ 11. A break in a bone

_____Shin Splint_____ 12. An overuse injury common among runners and aggressive walkers

Scoliosis
Shin Splint
Osteoporosis
Fracture
Dislocation

Activity 61
Use with Chapter 16, Lesson 2

The Muscular System

Using words and terms from your textbook, complete the following sentences.

1. Your muscular system is the group of structures that gives your body parts the power to _____ move _____.

2. The muscles attached to bones that enable you to move are called _____ skeletal _____ muscles.

3. Your _____ smooth _____ muscles are found in organs, blood vessels, and glands.

4. Involuntary muscles found only in the walls of your heart are _____ cardiac _____ muscles.

5. Muscle movement is triggered by _____ messages or impulses _____.

6. Before exercising you should always _____ warm _____ up.

7. The best way to keep your muscles toned is to _____ eat _____ well and keep _____ active _____.

8. When you lift something heavy, never _____ bend _____ over.

9. Sore muscles are a _____ temporary _____ condition.

10. Muscle strain is usually a result of _____ overworking _____ the muscle.

Chapter 16

Activity 62
Use with Chapter 16, Lesson 3

Your Circulatory System

Imagine that you have been asked to answer questions in a health class about the circulatory system because you are an expert in this area. Write your responses to these questions.

1. What is the circulatory system?

   The circulatory system is a group of organs and tissues that move essential supplies to

   body cells and remove their waste products.

2. What is the difference between veins and arteries?

   Veins are blood vessels that carry blood from the body back to the heart. Arteries are

   blood vessels that carry blood away from the heart to other parts of the body.

3. What is blood made up of?

   Blood is made up of nearly equal parts of solids and liquids. The liquid part, plasma, is about

   92 percent water. The solids in blood consist of blood cells and cell parts called platelets.

4. What is the difference between white blood cells and red blood cells?

   Red blood cells carry oxygen to cells and carbon dioxide away from them. White blood

   cells carry germ fighters from the immune system to needed areas of the body.

5. What is the job of platelets?

   Platelets help blood clot at the site of a wound.

   _____

6. How can I keep my circulatory system healthy?

   You can keep the circulatory system healthy by staying active with regular exercise, limiting

   the amount of fat in your eating plan, avoiding tobacco, and learning healthy ways to

   manage stress.

Chapter 16

Activity 63
Use with Chapter 16, Lesson 4

Your Respiratory System

Imagine that you are on a quiz show. One of the categories is the human respiratory system. The quiz show host presents an answer. You have to write a question.

1. **Answer:** You would not be able to eat without having this flap of tissue that covers your trachea when you swallow.

   Question: What is the epiglottis?

2. **Answer:** It's here that oxygen is transferred to the blood and carbon dioxide is removed.

   Question: Where are the lungs?

3. **Answer:** These are microscopic air sacs in the lungs where carbon dioxide is exchanged with oxygen.

   Question: What are alveoli?

4. **Answer:** This disease, in which alveoli are damaged or destroyed, causes serious breathing difficulties.

   Question: What is emphysema?

5. **Answer:** They are respiratory problems that are strongly linked to smoking.

   Question: What are emphysema and lung cancer?

6. **Answer:** This passage, also called the windpipe, directs air to the lungs.

   Question: What is the trachea?

7. **Answer:** This is where air enters and leaves the body.

   Question: What are the nose and mouth?

8. **Answer:** This large dome-shaped muscle separates the lungs from the abdomen.

   Question: What is the diaphragm?

Chapter 16

Activity 64
Use with Chapter 16, Lesson 5

Your Nervous System

Imagine that the parts of your nervous system can speak. In the space provided, identify each of the following parts of the nervous system by their descriptions.

_____Brain_____ 1. I am your body's message and control center.

Central Nervous System 2. I am a system that includes the brain and the spinal cord.

Peripheral Nervous System 3. I am a system that includes nerves that get information from all parts of the body.

_____Somatic_____ 4. I am a system dealing with actions that you control.

_____Automatic_____ 5. I am a system that deals with actions you do not control.

Traumatic Brain Injury 6. I am a condition caused by the brain being jarred and striking the inside of the skull.

_____Spinal Cord_____ 7. I am a column of nerve tissue about 18 inches long.

_____Vertebrae_____ 8. I am the bones that make up your spine.

_____Neurons_____ 9. I am specialized nerve cells that send and receive impulses.

_____Meninges_____ 10. I am the connective membranes in the spine.

Activity 65
Use with Chapter 16, Lesson 6

Caring for Your Digestive System

Below are guidelines for caring for your digestive system. Read the DO list to find out what you should do to care for your digestive system. Read the DON'T list to learn what to avoid.

DO
- Eat slowly
- Chew your food thoroughly
- Eat fiber-rich foods
- Drink eight 8-ounce glasses of water a day
- Get regular dental checkups
- Practice good oral hygiene

DON'T
- Forget to drink eight 8-ounce glasses of water a day
- Skip meals
- Rush through a meal
- Forget to chew food thoroughly
- Eat foods low in fiber

During the next three days, try to practice the Do's listed above and avoid the Don'ts. Monitor yourself three times a day—morning, afternoon, and evening. Use the chart below to show your progress. Write an *O* in the chart for each Do you practice during that part of the day. Write an *X* for each Don't.

	Day 1	Day 2	Day 3
Morning			
Afternoon			
Evening			

At the end of the three days, add the total number of *O*s and *X*s. Write these numbers below.

Number of *O*s _____   Number of *X*s _____

If there are more *O*s than *X*s, give yourself a reward. If there are more *X*s than *O*s, list three ways you can improve the care of your digestive system.

Answers will vary. Possible answers: Eat slowly. Chew your food thoroughly. Eat fiber-rich foods. Drink eight 8-ounce glasses of water a day. Get regular dental checkups. Practice good oral hygiene.

Chapter 16

Activity 66

Use with Chapter 16, Lesson 7

Your Endocrine System

Read each statement about the endocrine system. If the statement is true, write + on the line provided. If the statement is false, write 0 in the space provided and then rewrite the statement to make it true.

____+____ 1. A gland is a group of cells or an organ that secretes a *substance*.

_____

____0____ 2. The endocrine glands operate based on signals from the *heart*.

The endocrine glands operate based on signals from the brain or pituitary gland.

____+____ 3. The most common problem of the endocrine system is *diabetes*.

_____

____0____ 4. The chemicals secreted by the endocrine glands are called *pituitaries*.

The chemicals secreted by the endocrine glands are called hormones.

____0____ 5. Most cases of diabetes are *type 1*.

Most cases of diabetes are type 2.

____+____ 6. Regular physical activity and good nutrition help *endocrine health*.

_____

____+____ 7. Tiredness and depression are symptoms of *underactive* thyroids.

_____

____0____ 8. The endocrine glands are located in *one part of the body*.

The endocrine glands are located throughout the body.

____+____ 9. The adrenals, ovaries, and testes are all glands of the *endocrine* system.

_____

____0____ 10. People with underactive thyroids may experience weight *loss*.

People with underactive thyroids may experience weight gain.

Chapter 16

Activity 67
Use with Chapter 16, Lesson 8

Your Reproductive System

Match each definition in the left column with the correct term from the right column. Write the letter of the term in the space provided.

__b__ 1. Process by which one mature egg is released each month

__h__ 2. When the lining of the uterus, an unfertilized egg, and some blood flow out of the body

__j__ 3. Organ that receives and nourishes a fertilized egg

__f__ 4. Occurs when an internal organ pushes against or through a surrounding cavity wall

__c__ 5. When a male sperm cell joins with a female egg cell

__g__ 6. The male reproductive glands

__a__ 7. Forceful muscular contractions during which semen exits the penis

__d__ 8. Hormonal changes that occur in females from the beginning of one menstruation to the next

__e__ 9. The persistent inability to get pregnant

__i__ 10. The mixture of fluids and sperm

a. Ejaculation

b. Ovulation

c. Fertilization

d. Menstrual cycle

e. Infertility

f. Hernia

g. Testes

h. Menstruation

i. Semen

j. Uterus

Chapter 16

Applying Health Skills

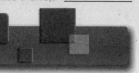

Accessing Information

Body Systems

In this chapter you have learned about the systems of the body. Research and prepare a fact sheet on a specific body system or part of a body system.

1. Choose a body system or part of a body system that you would like to learn more about. For example, if you have a friend with diabetes, you might want to learn more about the endocrine system. Name the body system or body system part that you have chosen.

   _____

2. Read about that body system or body system part in reliable print and/or Internet sources. On the lines below, record at least three facts you did not know before you began your research. Note the source where you found each fact.

   _____

   _____

   _____

   _____

   _____

   _____

   _____

   _____

   _____

Chapter 16

Chapter 17 Study Guide
Growth and Development

> ### Study Tips
> ✔ Read the chapter objectives.
> ✔ Look up any unfamiliar words.
> ✔ Read the questions below before you read the chapter.

   As you read the chapter, answer the following questions. Later you can use this guide to review the information in the chapter.

Lesson 1

1. What is fertilization?

Fertilization is the joining together of a male sperm cell and a female egg cell.

_____

_____

2. What is the uterus?

The uterus is a pear-shaped organ inside a female's body where the embryo is protected

and nourished.

_____

3. What occurs in stages two and three of the birth process?

In stage two of the birth process, the cervix continues to open. The contractions are

very strong. They happen more often. The contractions finally push the baby through

the cervix. The baby comes out of the mother's body. In stage three, the contractions

keep going until they push the placenta out of the uterus. The placenta can cause an

infection if it does not leave the body.

_____

_____

Chapter 17 Study Guide
Growth and Development

Lesson 2

4. What is a genetic disorder? Name two examples of genetic disorders.

A genetic disorder is a disorder caused partly or completely by a defect in genes. This is when one or both parents carry a gene with a flaw. Down syndrome is a genetic disorder caused by having an extra chromosome. People with this disorder have certain facial features and disabilities. Sickle cell anemia is a blood disorder caused by an abnormal gene. This disorder is having abnormally shaped red blood cells that cause pain in the bones and joints. It also blocks blood vessels.

5. What is prenatal care?

Prenatal care includes steps taken to provide for the health of a pregnant female and her baby.

6. How can alcohol use during pregnancy lead to birth defects?

When a pregnant female drinks alcohol, it enters her blood. It goes into the blood of her baby. This can lead to fetal alcohol syndrome (FAS). FAS causes physical and mental problems in children whose mothers drank alcohol when they were pregnant.

Lesson 3

7. What are the eight stages of development?

The eight stages of development include infancy, which is birth to 1 year; early childhood, which is 1 to 3 years; middle childhood, which is 3 to 5 years; late childhood, which is 6 to 11 years; adolescence, which is 12 to 18 years; young adulthood, which is 18 to 40 years; middle adulthood, which is 40 to 65 years; and maturity and old age, which is 65 years to death.

Chapter 17 Study Guide
Growth and Development

8. What occurs in the middle childhood stage of childhood?

This is a time of fast growth. The child becomes more coordinated. A child becomes

curious about the world, asks many questions, and uses his or her imagination. Playing

make-believe and copying adults helps the child gain social skills. Parents who encourage

activities and questions build the child's self-esteem. The child jumps and hops and

draws simple shapes.

9. What are some of the physical changes female adolescents experience?

Answers may include the following: Breasts develop. Hips get wider. Uterus and ovaries

enlarge. Ovulation occurs, and menstruation begins. Body fat increases. Hormone pro-

duction increases. Growth spurts occur. Acne may appear. Sweat increases. Pubic hair

appears. Underarm hair appears. Most permanent teeth are in.

Lesson 4

10. What are some things people do in middle adulthood?

Answers may include the following: Many people want to advance in their jobs. Many

people are raising their children. Many people are interested in helping the community

by volunteering or working with a charity. Many people are planning for their retirement.

11. What are some things people do in late adulthood?

Answers may include the following: Many people look forward to retirement. They want

to do things they did not have time to do when they were working and raising their chil-

dren. Some people continue to work, and some change careers. Many people stay active

and volunteer in the community.

12. What is the difference between chronological age and social age?

Chronological age is age measured in years. Social age is age measured by your lifestyle

and the connections you have with others.

Chapter 17

Activity 68
Use with Chapter 17, Lesson 1

New Life

Write the correct title from the list below on each numbered answer line. Then arrange the steps in each lettered list in the correct order.

Titles:

The Birth Process

Fertilization and Early Growth

Fetal Development

1. ____Fertilization and Early Growth____

____c____ **a.** The fertilized cluster of cells attaches itself to the wall of the uterus.

____d____ **b.** The placenta begins to provide nourishment to the developing fetus.

____b____ **c.** The fertilized cell begins to divide.

____a____ **d.** A sperm cell joins with an egg cell.

2. _____Fetal Development_____

____a____ **a.** The heart, brain, and lungs begin to form.

____c____ **b.** The arms and legs can move freely.

____b____ **c.** The heart is beating.

____d____ **d.** Body organs have developed to function on their own.

3. _____The Birth Process_____

____d____ **a.** Contractions push the placenta out of the mother's body.

____a____ **b.** Mild contractions begin.

____b____ **c.** The cervix opens to a width of about 4 inches.

____c____ **d.** The baby is born.

Chapter 17

Activity 69
Use with Chapter 17, Lesson 2

Heredity and Environment

Imagine that you are on a quiz show. One of the categories is "Heredity and Environment." The quiz show host presents an answer. You have to write a question.

1. **Answer:** These threadlike structures are found within the nucleus of a cell that carry the codes for inherited traits.

   Question: What are chromosomes? _____

2. **Answer:** This is the sum total of a person's surroundings.

   Question: What is environment? _____

3. **Answer:** During a prenatal visit, a woman's doctor may use this technology, which uses sound waves to form a picture of the fetus.

   Question: What is ultrasound? _____

4. **Answer:** These are abnormalities present at birth that cause physical or mental disability or death.

   Question: What are birth defects? _____

5. **Answer:** This is a doctor whose specialty is the care of pregnant women and their fetuses.

   Question: What is an obstetrician? _____

6. **Answer:** This occurs in a baby when the baby's genes supplied by one or both parents are abnormal or changed in some way.

   Question: What is a genetic disorder? _____

7. **Answer:** These are physical characteristics, such as eye color, hair color, or body shape passed on from parents to their children.

   Question: What are traits? _____

8. **Answer:** These are the basic units of heredity.

   Question: What are genes? _____

Activity 70
Use with Chapter 17, Lesson 3

The Stages of Growth

Even though everyone grows at a slightly different rate, each individual passes through certain stages of development. Read the description of each person below. Identify the developmental stage by writing *I* for infancy, *E* for early childhood, *M* for middle childhood, *L* for late childhood, or *A* for adolescence.

E   1. Brendan has just learned to climb stairs. He feels proud of his accomplishment but does not understand why his mother was upset when she saw him climbing the stairs in their home by himself.

M   2. Hannah would rather run than walk. She loves to pretend she is a monster that growls and chases people. She is very curious about the world around her and constantly asks her parents, "Why?" about everything she sees.

I   3. Toshio is beginning to recognize the people around him. He smiles when he sees his mother's face and laughs when he is tickled. He wants to touch everything he can reach.

L   4. Andre has recently developed a great interest in jigsaw puzzles. After many tries, he has successfully put together his first large puzzle all by himself.

A   5. Cory is beginning to develop a sense of his own identity. He is often irritated for no reason and has grown several inches in the last year.

M   6. Jamal has started following his father around the house and imitating what he does. He wants to help him with everything, so his father bought him a play set of tools to use while he works on his own projects.

E   7. Kendra has recently added several new words to her vocabulary, but her favorite word is still no. She is able to ask for what she wants now, using one to three words at a time.

L   8. In the last few weeks, Sierra has made several new friends. They sit together at the lunch table and play handball at recess.

A   9. Stephen is teased by his family for his cracking, changing voice, and he thinks it is funny too. He has applied for a part-time job after school, and is looking forward to more independence.

Chapter 17

Activity 71

Growing Older and Staying Well

After we become adults, we pass through three basic stages in the aging process: early adulthood, middle adulthood, and late adulthood. Each stage is marked by certain milestones, and how well we age depends on a variety of physical, mental and emotional, and social factors.

Complete the charts below by identifying some of these milestones and factors. Then answer the questions that follow.

Stage of Adulthood	Milestones
Early Adulthood	Begin to work for a living, get married, and start having children
Middle Adulthood	Advance in a job; raise children; gain satisfaction from helping young people; face challenges of building a career, caring for home and children, and caring for aged parents
Late Adulthood	Look forward to retirement, pursue new interests, change careers, stay active by doing volunteer work in the community

Health Triangle	Factors that can affect aging
Physical Health	Stay physically active, get enough rest, eat sensibly
Mental/Emotional Health	Keep mentally active by reading and working, take on new challenges
Social Health	Maintain close contact with family and friends, become involved in community programs that utilize one's talents and life experiences

1. What are three different ways in which age can be measured?

   Three different ways that age can be measured are chronological age, biological age, or

   social age.

2. Why is it important for adults to pay attention to all three sides of the health triangle?

   Paying attention to all three sides of the health triangle can help make the later years

   healthier and more rewarding and productive.

Chapter 17

Chapter 17 Health Inventory

Becoming an Adult

Read the statements below. In the space at the left, write *yes* **if the
statement describes you, or** *no* **if it does not describe you.**

_____ 1. I think that my chances of reaching my goals for the future are good.

_____ 2. I am now preparing for the responsibilities and challenges of adulthood.

_____ 3. I expect to work for what I want rather than just have things happen to me.

_____ 4. I think it is important to be involved in the community even though I am
still in my teen years.

_____ 5. I am good at accepting changes in my life.

_____ 6. I am beginning to think about the type of work I am interested in doing
after I finish high school.

_____ 7. I get my school assignments completed on time.

_____ 8. I can make my own decisions without giving in to peer pressure.

_____ 9. I carry out my responsibilities without being reminded.

_____ 10. I know what people like and dislike about me.

_____ 11. I expect to be mentally and physically active throughout my life.

_____ 12. My behavior reflects my personal standards and values.

_____ 13. I believe that good health is important to the aging process.

_____ 14. Staying mentally active is just as important as staying physically active.

_____ 15. I intend to stick with the healthy eating and exercise habits that I am
developing in my teen years.

Score yourself:

Write the number of *yes* answers here. ⬜

12–15: Excellent

8–11: Good

Fewer than 8: Adolescence is a time to begin taking more responsibility for your actions.
How can you improve in this area?

Chapter 17

Chapter 18 Study Guide
Communicable Diseases

Study Tips

✔ Read the chapter objectives.

✔ Look up any unfamiliar words.

✔ Read the questions below before you read the chapter.

As you read the chapter, answer the following questions. Later you can use this guide to review the information in the chapter.

Lesson 1

1. What are four common types of pathogens?

Four common types of pathogens are viruses, bacteria, fungi, and protozoa.

_____

_____

2. Name four ways pathogens spread.

Pathogens spread through direct and indirect contact with others, through contact with

contaminated food and water, and through contact with animals or insects.

_____

_____

Lesson 2

3. What is the function of the immune system?

The immune system's function is to fight off bacteria, viruses, and other pathogens. It is

a combination of body defenses made up of the cells, tissues, and organs that fight off

pathogens and disease. The immune system has two main responses—the nonspecific

response and the specific response. Together these responses provide immunity.

4. What is the lymphatic system?

The lymphatic system is a secondary circulatory system that helps the body fight

pathogens and maintains its fluid balance.

Chapter 18

Chapter 18 Study Guide
Communicable Diseases

Lesson 3

5. How are the cold and the flu similar and different?

Both the cold and the flu are common communicable diseases. They can also be spread

through direct and indirect contact. Unlike the flu, the common cold does not have a

vaccine. The flu can also be serious, whereas the common cold rarely becomes a

serious condition.

6. How is hepatitis spread?

Hepatitis A is spread though food or water that has been contaminated by human

waste. Hepatitis B and C are usually spread through contact with contaminated blood

or other body fluids. Vaccines can prevent people from contracting hepatitis A and B.

Medications can help treat those infected with hepatitis C.

Lesson 4

7. What are sexually transmitted diseases sometimes called?

Sexually transmitted diseases are sometimes called sexually transmitted infections (STIs).

8. What are three sexually transmitted diseases caused by bacteria?

One sexually transmitted disease caused by bacteria is chlamydia. Another sexually

transmitted disease caused by bacteria is gonorrhea. A third sexually transmitted disease

caused by bacteria is syphilis. The advanced stages of all three are very serious.

9. What is the best way to avoid getting a sexually transmitted disease?

The best way to avoid contracting a sexually transmitted disease is by practicing

abstinence.

Lesson 5

10. What is a carrier?

A carrier is a person who appears healthy but is infected with HIV and can pass it on to

others. A person may be infected for ten years or more before starting to show symptoms

of AIDS.

Chapter 18 Study Guide
Communicable Diseases

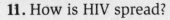

11. How is HIV spread?

HIV is spread from person to person through contact with specific body fluids. These

fluids include sperm, fluid from the vagina, blood, and breast milk. One way HIV

spreads is through sexual contact with an infected person. Another way HIV is spread

is through sharing needles with an infected person.

12. What are three ways HIV infection and AIDS can be prevented?

One way HIV and AIDS can be prevented is by practicing abstinence. Another way is

avoiding drugs and alcohol. A third way HIV and AIDS can be prevented is by avoiding

shared needles.

_____

_____

_____

_____

_____

_____

_____

Chapter 18

Activity 72
Use with Chapter 18, Lesson 1

Preventing Communicable Diseases

There are various ways to prevent the spread of communicable diseases. Read the following situations. Write the unhealthy behavior in each situation below. Then write the healthful behavior that will help defend against disease.

Situation 1

Dylan's brother, Thomas, has had a bad cold for the last week. Dylan made a sandwich for lunch while Thomas sat at the table eating a bowl of soup. "Can I have some of your soup?" Dylan asked.

To prevent the spread of pathogens, people should not share utensils. Dylan should get his

own bowl and spoon, and serve himself some soup.

Situation 2

Nicole had the flu for two days. After the second day at home, she did not feel much better, but refused to be home another day. A big test was approaching and Nicole wanted to be sure she would be there for the review. She asked her father to cancel the doctor's appointment he made and got ready to go to school.

Nicole should not go to school to protect others from infection. She should stay home until

she feels well and go to that doctor's appointment.

Situation 3

At the neighborhood barbecue, Shakira could not wait to have a hamburger off the grill. When she took a large bite, she realized the inside of the burger was still very red and not warm. However, Shakira was so hungry she decided to keep eating.

The meat is undercooked. Shakira could get sick from eating undercooked meat. She should

take it back to the grill.

Situation 4

Annie and Michael were walking home on a hot August day. They were both wearing shorts and t-shirts, but couldn't seem to cool off. Michael suggested they take a shortcut through the shaded forest because the woods were much cooler than the sidewalk. The woods were very dense and overgrown, but Annie agreed.

Annie and Michael should avoid the woods because they are not wearing pants and

long-sleeved shirts. They are putting themselves at risk for ticks and other insect bites.

Chapter 18

Activily 13
Use with Chapter 18, Lesson 2

The Body's Defenses Against Infection

The body has three levels of defense against possible invading pathogens. Complete the following chart to show these levels of defense.

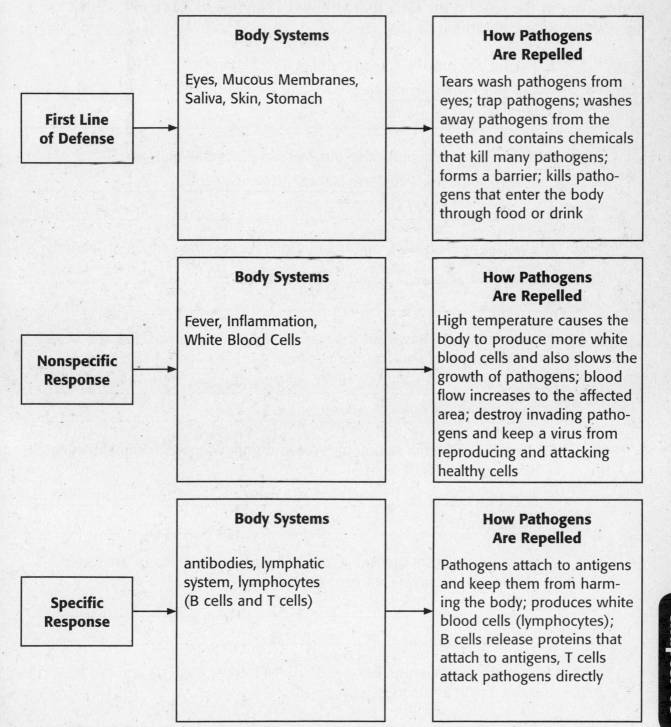

First Line of Defense →

Body Systems

Eyes, Mucous Membranes, Saliva, Skin, Stomach

→ **How Pathogens Are Repelled**

Tears wash pathogens from eyes; trap pathogens; washes away pathogens from the teeth and contains chemicals that kill many pathogens; forms a barrier; kills pathogens that enter the body through food or drink

Nonspecific Response →

Body Systems

Fever, Inflammation, White Blood Cells

→ **How Pathogens Are Repelled**

High temperature causes the body to produce more white blood cells and also slows the growth of pathogens; blood flow increases to the affected area; destroy invading pathogens and keep a virus from reproducing and attacking healthy cells

Specific Response →

Body Systems

antibodies, lymphatic system, lymphocytes (B cells and T cells)

→ **How Pathogens Are Repelled**

Pathogens attach to antigens and keep them from harming the body; produces white blood cells (lymphocytes); B cells release proteins that attach to antigens, T cells attack pathogens directly

Chapter 18

Activity 74
Use with Chapter 18, Lesson 3

Communicable Diseases

Some of the following statements about communicable diseases are facts and others are not. Classify each statement by writing *true* or *false* in the space at the left. On the lines that follow the statements, correct the ones you have identified as false.

_____False_____ **1.** The flu can only be spread through direct contact.

The flu can be spread through direct or indirect contact.
_____

_____False_____ **2.** Only certain communicable diseases have a contagious period.

Every communicable disease has a contagious period.
_____

_____True_____ **3.** Chicken pox, measles, and mumps all have specific contagious periods.

_____
_____

_____False_____ **4.** Hepatitis, also known as "the kissing disease," is spread through contact with the saliva of an infected person.

Mononucleosis is known as "the kissing disease" and is spread through

contact with the saliva of an infected person.

_____False_____ **5.** Hepatitis A is most commonly spread through contact with contaminated blood or other body fluids.

Hepatitis A is spread through food and water that has been contaminated by

human waste.

_____True_____ **6.** Since tuberculosis can spread easily though the air, people are tested periodically to see if they have the disease.

_____
_____

_____True_____ **7.** Pneumonia and strep throat are both caused by bacteria and can be treated with antibiotics.

_____
_____

Chapter 18

Activity 75
Use with Chapter 18, Lesson 4

Understanding Sexually Transmitted Diseases

In the space, write the word(s) from the list that will best complete each statement.

1. Most STDs are spread only through _____ **sexual** _____ contact.

2. STDs can _____ **recur** _____ because the body does not build up an immunity to them.

3. _____ **Genital herpes** _____ can be passed on to another person even when the blisters are not present.

4. If _____ **gonorrhea** _____ is left untreated, it can infect other parts of the body, such as the heart, and cause fertility problems for men and women.

5. Like genital herpes and chlamydia, _____ **HPV** _____ is often a silent disease.

6. During the advanced stage, _____ **syphilis** _____ can cause mental disorders, blindness, heart problems, paralysis, and even death.

gonorrhea

genital Herpes

HPV

sexual

syphilis

recur

Answer the following questions about sexually transmitted diseases. Write your answers on the lines provided.

7. Can you tell if someone has an STD by his or her appearance?

No, you cannot tell if someone has an STD by his or her appearance.

8. What are the similarities between genital herpes and genital warts?

Genital herpes and genital warts are both caused by viruses. Both are transmitted by skin-to-skin contact and can be treated, but not cured.

9. What is the best way to avoid getting an STD?

The best way to avoid getting an STD is to abstain from sexual activity.

10. What can you do to spread awareness of STDs?

Share information about abstinence and the risks STDs pose.

Chapter 18

Activity 76
Use with Chapter 18, Lesson 5

HIV/AIDS Facts and Myths

Some of the statements below are facts and others are not. Classify each by writing *fact* or *myth* on the line at the left.

___myth___ **1.** One way to get HIV is to give blood.

___fact___ **2.** Pricking the skin with contaminated needles can spread HIV.

___myth___ **3.** People can catch HIV from infected insects.

___fact___ **4.** Being infected with HIV makes it possible for other pathogens to attack the body.

___myth___ **5.** Hugging someone who is infected with HIV can spread the disease.

___fact___ **6.** AIDS does not have a cure.

___fact___ **7.** HIV attacks and weakens the body's immune system.

___fact___ **8.** Unborn babies can get HIV from their mothers.

___myth___ **9.** One way to get HIV is to touch something an infected person has touched.

___myth___ **10.** You can get HIV by swimming in the same pool as an infected person.

___fact___ **11.** Tattoos and body piercings can spread HIV if performed with contaminated needles.

___fact___ **12.** Those infected with HIV can spread HIV even though they show no signs of the virus themselves.

13. Imagine you are in charge of informing the public about HIV/AIDS. On the lines below, list three ways you could get the facts to the public.

Answers can include: public service messages on radio and television, in magazines

and newspapers; posters in public places; mailings to households in the United States;

public speakers to discuss HIV/AIDS; AIDS education in schools; work with community

and volunteer organizations.

_____

_____

Chapter 18

Applying Health Skills

Practicing Healthful Behaviors

Preventing the Spread of Disease

With other students, create and perform a skit about ways to prevent the spread of pathogens.

Answers will vary. Possible responses provided.

1. With your partner or group, list at least five ways to prevent the spread of pathogens.

   Keep your hands clean. Avoid contact with people infected with a communicable disease.

   Never share eating or drinking utensils. Do not share toothbrushes or other personal

   hygiene items. Avoid touching your mouth, nose, and eyes. Do not bite your nails.

   Handle and prepare food safely. Wipe counters thoroughly.

2. Plan a short skit in which the characters discuss or demonstrate ways to prevent the spread of pathogens. Use the ideas you have listed above. Write a brief description of the situation, the characters, and the action of your skit.

   Answers will vary.

3. Together, practice acting out your skit.

4. Perform your skit for the rest of the class.

Chapter 18

Chapter 19 Study Guide
Noncommunicable Diseases

Study Tips
✔ Read the chapter objectives.

✔ Look up any unfamiliar words.

✔ Read the questions below before you read the chapter.

As you read the chapter, answer the following questions. Later you can use this guide to review the information in the chapter.

Lesson 1

1. What are *congenital disorders?*

Congenital disorders are disorders that are present when a baby is born.

2. Name four risk factors for disease that you cannot control.

Four risk factors for disease that you cannot control are heredity, age, gender, and

ethnic group.

Lesson 2

3. What is the most common form of cancer?

Skin cancer is the most common form of cancer.

4. Define *carcinogens*.

Carcinogens are substances that cause cancer.

5. What are the ABCDs when looking for a change in a mole or other skin formation?

The ABCDs when looking for a change in a mole or other skin formation are: Asymmetry,

Border, Color, and Diameter.

Chapter 19 Study Guide
Noncommunicable Diseases

Lesson 3

6. What is the difference between arteriosclerosis and atherosclerosis?

Arteriosclerosis is a group of disorders in which arteries harden and become more rigid.

Atherosclerosis is a form of arteriosclerosis in which fatty substances in the blood build

up on the walls of the arteries.

7. How can being physically active help prevent heart disease?

Being overweight puts you at risk for heart disease because the extra weight puts strain

on the heart and makes it work harder.

Lesson 4

8. What health concerns can be caused by diabetes?

Kidney disorders, blindness, and heart disease are all health concerns that can be caused

by diabetes.

9. How can physical activity and rest reduce the symptoms of arthritis?

Physical activity and rest can reduce the symptoms of arthritis by reducing swelling in the

joints and increasing flexibility in the affected areas.

Lesson 5

10. What is an allergy?

An allergy is an extreme sensitivity to a substance.

11. Name three common triggers for asthma.

Three common triggers for asthma are (any three): mold, dust, pollen, pets, and other

allergens; strenuous or energetic activity; paint and gas fumes; smoke; smog; air

pollution; colds, the flu, and other respiratory infections; extreme weather changes;

and strong emotions.

Activity 77
Use with Chapter 19, Lesson 1

The Truth About Noncommunicable Diseases

Some of the following statements about noncommunicable diseases are facts and others are not. Classify each statement by writing *true* or *false* in the space at the left. On the lines that follow the statements, correct the ones you have identified as false.

_____true_____ 1. Multiple sclerosis is an example of a degenerative disease.

_____

_____

_____false_____ 2. All disorders that are present when a baby is born are called degenerative disorders.

All disorders that are present when a baby is born are called congenital

disorders.

_____false_____ 3. The causes of most birth defects are known.

The causes of most birth defects are unknown.

_____

_____true_____ 4. Chronic diseases are present either continuously or on and off over a long period of time.

_____

_____

_____false_____ 5. While it is hard to determine who will develop a disease, researchers have found that behavior does not affect a person's chance of developing a disease.

Researchers have found that certain risk factors affect a person's chance of

developing a disease.

_____true_____ 6. Smog is one environmental factor that can cause respiratory disease.

_____

_____

Activity 78
Use with Chapter 19, Lesson 2

Understanding Cancer

Each patient described below is being treated for cancer. In each case, write the missing term in the space to the left of the case study.

Surgery	Remission	Recurrence
Chemotherapy	Biopsy	Radiation therapy

1. Patient A is undergoing ____radiation therapy____, a treatment that uses X rays or other forms of radiation to kill cancer cells.

2. Doctors have discovered a suspicious lump on Patient B and have decided to perform a _____biopsy_____ on the tissue.

3. ____Chemotherapy____ helped Patient C fight cancers that had already spread through the body.

4. Patient D's cancer treatment has been very successful. The doctors tell her the cancer is in _____remission_____.

5. Even though Patient E's cancer was in remission, a _____recurrence_____ has occurred.

6. The cancer in Patient F has not spread to new parts of the body and has remained in one place. Doctors think _____surgery_____ will be most effective in removing the cancerous cells from the body.

Do you know how to reduce the risk of cancer? Next to each factor, write a plus (+) sign if it can help keep your body healthy. Write a minus (–) sign if it does not reduce the risk of cancer.

___–___ 7. Cigarette smoking

___+___ 8. Limiting sun exposure

___–___ 9. Eat a high intake of saturated fats

___+___ 10. Performing self-examinations

___+___ 11. Regular physical activity

Activity 79
Use with Chapter 19, Lesson 3

Heart and Circulatory Problems

Some of the following statements about heart and circulatory problems are facts and others are not. Classify each statement by writing *true* or *false* in the space at the left. On the lines that follow the statements, correct the ones you have identified as false.

_____false_____ 1. Arteriosclerosis is a condition in which the pressure of the blood on the walls of the blood vessels stays at a level that is higher than normal.

Hypertension is a condition in which the pressure of the blood on the walls

of the blood vessels stays at a level that is higher than normal.

_____true_____ 2. If the space in the coronary arteries narrows, the limited space can stop the heart from getting enough oxygen.

_____

_____

_____true_____ 3. High blood pressure can cause a heart attack or stroke.

_____

_____

_____false_____ 4. A heart attack is a serious condition that occurs when an artery of the brain breaks or becomes blocked.

A stroke is a serious condition that occurs when an artery of the brain breaks

or becomes blocked.

_____false_____ 5. Smoking cigarettes can help you prevent heart disease, heart attacks, hypertension, and strokes.

Smoking cigarettes can lead to heart disease, heart attacks, hypertension, and

strokes.

_____true_____ 6. An angioplasty is a way to open arteries that become blocked.

_____

_____

Activity 80
Use with Chapter 19, Lesson 4

Diabetes and Arthritis

Identify each term in the column on the right by matching it with the correct description in the column on the left. Write the term in the space provided.

__Rheumatoid Arthritis__   **1.** A chronic disease characterized by pain, inflammation, swelling, and stiffness of the joints

__Type 2 diabetes__   **2.** A condition in which the body cannot effectively use the insulin it produces

__Insulin__   **3.** A protein made in the pancreas that regulates the level of glucose in the blood

__Diabetes__   **4.** A disease that prevents the body from converting food into energy

__Osteoarthritis__   **5.** A chronic disease that results from a breakdown in cartilage in the joints

__Type 1 diabetes__   **6.** A condition in which the immune system attacks insulin-producing cells in the pancreas

__Arthritis__   **7.** A disease of the joints marked by painful swelling and stiffness

Type 2 diabetes

Osteoarthritis

Diabetes

Arthritis

Insulin

Rheumatoid Arthritis

Type 1 diabetes

Answer the following questions about diabetes and arthritis. Write your answers on the lines provided.

8. Explain the difference between type 1 and type 2 diabetes in relation to insulin.

In type 1, the pancreas produces little or no insulin to balance the glucose in the blood.

In type 2, the body is not able to effectively use the insulin it produces.

9. What are some ways to manage arthritis?

Physical activity and rest, a balanced eating plan, joint protection, heat and cold treatments,

medication, massage, surgery and joint replacement are ways to manage arthritis.

Chapter 19

Activity 81
Use with Chapter 19, Lesson 5

Allergies and Asthma

Fill in the chart by listing six common allergens and one common source for that allergen. Answers will vary. Possible answers given.

Allergen	Common Sources for Allergen
1. Food	Peanuts
2. Household dust	Feather duster
3. Insects	Yellow jackets
4. Pets	Cats
5. Plants	Poison ivy
6. Pollens	Flowers, Trees, Grasses, Weeds

7. Define *hives*.

Hives are raised bumps on the skin that are very itchy.

8. What are three basic tips for managing allergies?

Avoid the allergen; take medication; get injections.

9. What can trigger an asthma attack?

Allergens, physical activity, respiratory infections, irritants, fumes, stressful events, and

vigorous laughing can trigger an asthma attack.

10. What are three strategies people with asthma can use to help avoid asthma attacks?

People with asthma should monitor the condition, manage the environment, manage

stress, take medication.

Chapter 19 Health Inventory

Prevention and Your Health

Do you follow the good health habits that will help protect you from getting noncommunicable diseases? Use the questions below to find out. Write *yes* or *no* in the space at the left of each statement.

_____ 1. Do you know your family's medical history?

_____ 2. Do you watch for the seven warning signs of cancer?

_____ 3. Do you limit the amount of fat you eat?

_____ 4. Do you perform regular self-examinations for breast or testicular cancer?

_____ 5. Do you limit the amount of salt you eat?

_____ 6. Do you use sunscreen to protect your skin from the sun?

_____ 7. Do you eat plenty of whole grains, fruits, and vegetables every day?

_____ 8. Do you know the warning signs of melanoma?

_____ 9. Do you avoid using drugs?

_____ 10. Do you maintain a healthy weight?

_____ 11. Do you avoid using tobacco products?

_____ 12. Do you engage in regular physical activity?

_____ 13. Do you get 8 to 9 hours of sleep each night?

_____ 14. Do you deal with stress in a healthy way?

_____ 15. Do you avoid using alcohol?

Score yourself:

Write the number of *yes* answers here. ☐

12–15: Good for you! You are taking good care of yourself!

8–11: Fair. You can do better!

Fewer than 8: Remember only a healthy body can fight disease. Review Chapter 19 again to learn about the ways you can prevent diseases.

Chapter 20 Study Guide
Safety and Emergencies

Study Tips

✔ Read the chapter objectives.

✔ Look up any unfamiliar words.

✔ Read the questions below before you read the chapter.

As you read the chapter, answer the following questions. Later you can use this guide to review the information in the chapter.

Lesson 1

1. What are some ways you can prevent electric shock at home?

Answers may include the following: Any broken appliance should be unplugged. Replace broken or frayed electrical cords. Do not run cords under rugs. Keep appliances and cords away from water.

2. What are some safety precautions for keeping guns in the home?

Answers may include the following: Guns should be kept unloaded. Keep them in a locked cabinet. Keep bullets in a separate locked cabinet. Train anyone who will use the guns. Hold a gun as if it were loaded. Never point a gun at anyone.

Lesson 2

3. What are some ways to stay safe when you ride a bike?

Answers may include the following: Wear a helmet. Follow the rules of the road. Ride with traffic. Obey traffic signals and signs. Practice defensive driving.

Chapter 20 Study Guide
Safety and Emergencies

4. What are some water safety rules you should follow to prevent drowning?

Answers may include the following: Learn how to swim. Never swim alone. Wear a life jacket during water activities. Swim parallel to shore if you are in a strong current. Only dive into water that is deeper than 9 feet and free of any obstacles.

Lesson 3

5. What is a tornado?

A tornado is a whirling, funnel-shaped windstorm that may drop from the sky to the ground.

6. What is a blizzard?

A blizzard is a very heavy snowstorm with winds up to 45 miles per hour.

Lesson 4

7. Define *universal precautions*.

Universal precautions are actions taken to prevent the spread of disease by treating all blood as if it were contaminated.

8. What are some ways you can prepare yourself for an emergency?

Answers may include the following: Keep a list of emergency numbers near the phone. Keep first-aid kits in the home and car.

9. What are the four steps to take for most emergencies?

Identify the signs of an emergency, take action, call for help, and provide care until help arrives.

Chapter 20 Study Guide
Safety and Emergencies

Chapter 20

Lesson 5

10. What do the letters in the P.R.I.C.E. method stand for? What type of injuries can be treated using this method?

   The letters in P.R.I.C.E. stand for protect, rest, ice, compress, and elevate. This method can

   be used to treat minor sprains.

   _____

11. What are some ways you can help a person who faints?

   Answers may include: Check the person's airway. Raise the legs above the level of the

   head. Loosen any tight clothing. Call for help if the person does not regain consciousness

   in a minute. Start CPR. A head injury is not fainting. Call for medical help right away.

   Begin CPR if the person is not breathing.

12. What are heat cramps, and how should they be treated?

   Heat cramps are painful, involuntary muscle spasms that usually occur during strenuous

   exercise in hot weather. The person needs to rest, cool down, and drink water or a sports

   drink. Gentle stretching and massage may help.

   _____

Lesson 6

13. What are abdominal thrusts?

   Abdominal thrusts are quick upward pulls into the diaphragm to force out an obstruction

   blocking the airway.

   _____

14. What are some things that can cause a person to go into shock?

   Shock can result from injury, burns, severe infections, heat, poisoning, blood loss, and

   heart attack.

   _____

Activity 82
Use with Chapter 20, Lesson 1

Chapter 20

Being Safety Conscious

Read the statements below. Write *safe* on the line at the left if the statement describes a safety-conscious person. Write *unsafe* if the statement describes a person who is not safety conscious. Change each unsafe behavior to a safe one on the line following the statement.

___unsafe___   1. Jacob stores a loaded gun in his unlocked closet.

Jacob keeps his gun unloaded in a locked cabinet. _____

___unsafe___   2. Natalie tries to call attention to herself by taking unnecessary risks.

Natalie never tries to call attention to herself by taking unnecessary risks. _____

___safe___   3. Felicia's family practices fire drills regularly.

_____

___unsafe___   4. Taylor sometimes acts recklessly to impress her peers.

Taylor acts responsibly and considers her own safety. _____

___safe___   5. Will knows he has to be most careful when he is tired or upset.

_____

___safe___   6. Jorge is always aware of his surroundings and of possible hazards.

_____

___safe___   7. Fiona uses a step stool or a ladder when trying to reach high places.

_____

___unsafe___   8. Morgan often acts on impulse instead of planning ahead.

Morgan plans ahead instead of acting on impulse. _____

___unsafe___   9. Jeremy almost never cleans his stove, even when he spills food on it.

Jeremy cleans his stove often to avoid burns and fires. _____

___safe___   10. David takes responsibility for his own safety.

_____

Activity 83
Use with Chapter 20, Lesson 2

Staying Safe on the Road and Outdoors

Read the statements below. Identify each safe statement by writing *S* in the space at the left, and each unsafe statement by writing *U*.

___U___ 1. Tori is shivering in the cold rain, but she decides to continue jogging for another hour.

___S___ 2. Nicholas always uses his safety belt when he drives in a car.

___S___ 3. Kaya dresses for a cold day outside by wearing several layers of clothing.

___S___ 4. Emma and Thane agree to stay together during their hike up Willow Mountain.

___U___ 5. Maeve often rides a bicycle on the road at night without wearing reflective clothing or having reflectors on her bike.

___U___ 6. Although a thunderstorm is starting and he can see lightning in the distance, Ryan continues swimming in the lake.

___U___ 7. Before the rest of Anna's family gets up each morning, she exercises alone by swimming across Raven Lake.

___U___ 8. Brian hears someone calling for help from the deep end of the pool, so he jumps in to help even though he is not a strong swimmer.

___U___ 9. Cody and Jared dare each other to eat the berries of the plants they find along their hiking trail.

___S___ 10. Shoshana always wears a helmet when she rides her bike, even if she is just riding around the block near her house.

___S___ 11. Before Terrel dives into the pool, he checks the depth of the water.

___U___ 12. Although Alicia has been skiing only once, she agrees to try the expert slope with two of her friends, both of whom are advanced skiers.

___U___ 13. Abbey ignores the "Thin Ice" warning signs because she wants to practice her ice skating routine for the upcoming competition.

___U___ 14. Elvis refuses to wear a helmet when he skateboards because he says it interferes with his vision.

___U___ 15. If Azar is in a hurry, he crosses in the middle of the city street instead of the crosswalk.

Activity 84
Use with Chapter 20, Lesson 3

Weather Emergencies

On the lines provided, tell what you would do in each weather emergency described below.

1. You are at home, listening to the radio, when a tornado warning is announced. What would you do?

You should stay away from the windows; go to an inner hallway or room without

windows, like a bathroom or closet; get underneath a piece of sturdy furniture and

hold on to it, or cover yourself with a mattress, blanket, or clothing for protection.

2. The National Weather Service has issued a hurricane warning for your area. You are the only person at home, and you have been unable to reach other family members by telephone. What would you do?

You should close storm shutters or board up windows; bring inside any objects that

might be blown away, such as outdoor furniture or toys.

3. You are outdoors when a winter storm unexpectedly turns into a blizzard. What would you do?

You should wrap your scarf around your neck and mouth, cover your ears with a hat, and

keep your hands and fingers inside gloves and in your pockets. Stay close to a landmark

to find your way, or stay where you are until help arrives.

4. While walking home during a heavy rainstorm, you come to a stream that you usually walk across because it has stepping stones. However, the water is rising rapidly, and the current is much stronger than usual. What would you do?

Do not try to walk across. Head toward higher ground and find another way home that

avoids the stream.

5. Your house begins to shake, and you realize that an earthquake is taking place. What would you do?

Crouch under a sturdy desk or table against an interior wall, or in a strongly supported

doorway. Stay away from objects that might fall, shatter, or cave in. Cover your face with

your arms or a pillow.

Activity 85
Use with Chapter 20, Lesson 4

Basic First Aid

Answer the following questions about basic first aid.

1. What is first aid?

First aid is the immediate temporary care given to an injured or ill person until he or she

can get professional help.

2. Why is it important to know basic first aid?

It is important to know basic first aid because without warning, at any time or place, you

may find yourself in a position to give first aid.

3. What are universal precautions?

Universal precautions are actions taken to prevent the spread of disease by treating all

blood as if it were contaminated.

4. What are the four steps to take for most emergencies?

The four steps to take for most emergencies are: Recognize the signs of an emergency;

take action; call for help; provide care until help arrives.

5. When dialing 911 for an emergency, what should you remember
   to do?

Remember to stay calm. Describe the emergency to the operator and give a street

address or describe the location by using landmarks. Stay on the phone until the

operator tells you to hang up.

Activity 86
Use with Chapter 20, Lesson 5

Common Emergencies

You can effectively help someone who is hurt if you know how to give first aid in common emergencies. Read the list for each common emergency below. Check your knowledge by writing *X* on the line in front of each item that tells what you should do.

Sprains

_____ **1.** Move the injured part to keep it from becoming stiff.

__X__ **2.** Apply ice to reduce swelling and pain.

__X__ **3.** Elevate the sprained part above the level of the heart.

First-Degree Burns

__X__ **4.** Flush the burned area with cold water.

_____ **5.** Remove loose skin.

__X__ **6.** Loosely cover the burn with a sterile bandage.

Foreign Object in the Eye

__X__ **7.** Lightly touch the object with a moistened cotton swab.

__X__ **8.** Try to flush the object from the eye with clean water.

_____ **9.** Rub the eye vigorously.

Nosebleeds

_____ **10.** Have the person put his or her head down.

__X__ **11.** Pinch the nose for 5 to 10 minutes.

__X__ **12.** If bleeding continues, get medical help.

Insect Bites

__X__ **13.** Wash the affected area.

__X__ **14.** Apply ice or a cold pack to reduce pain and swelling.

_____ **15.** Leave the bite uncovered.

Poisoning

__X__ **16.** Call the nearest poison control center.

_____ **17.** Induce vomiting in all cases.

__X__ **18.** Be ready to provide information about the victim and the suspected poison.

Chapter 20

Activity 87
Use with Chapter 20, Lesson 6

Dealing with Life-Threatening Emergencies

Listed below are the steps that should be taken in certain life-threatening emergencies. Put the steps in the order in which they should be done by writing the correct letter in the space to the left. The first one in each group has been done for you.

Saving a Choking Adult

__c__ **1.** Quickly thrust inward and upward, as if trying to lift the person.

__d__ **2.** Repeat thrusts until the food or object is dislodged.

__a__ **3.** Stand behind the person and wrap your arms around his or her waist.

__b__ **4.** Make a fist with one hand, and place it just above the person's navel.

Treating a Person in Shock

__b__ **5.** Have the person lie down and raise the feet higher than the head.

__c__ **6.** Look for signs of shock, such as a weak, rapid pulse and shallow breathing.

__d__ **7.** Cover the person with a blanket or coat to keep him or her warm.

__a__ **8.** Loosen tight-fitting clothing.

Treating Severe Bleeding

__c__ **9.** Apply direct pressure to the wound, using a clean cloth.

__d__ **10.** Secure the cloth with a bandage or other material.

__b__ **11.** Raise the site of bleeding above the level of the heart.

__a__ **12.** Wash the wound with mild soap and water.

Giving CPR to an Adult

__a__ **13.** Look inside the victim's mouth. If you see anything blocking the airway, remove it.

__d__ **14.** Begin chest compressions.

__b__ **15.** Lay the person flat on a firm surface.

__c__ **16.** If victim is not breathing, begin rescue breathing.

Applying Health Skills

Refusal Skills

Staying Safe

With a partner, create a role-play about a teen who uses refusal skills to avoid unsafe behavior.

1. With your partner, choose a situation in which a teen is pressured to do something unsafe. Choose one of the situations in the boxes below, and put a check mark in that box. If you prefer, make up your own situation. Write a brief description of that situation in the empty box.

> Miguel has offered to teach Olivia how to skateboard. He says that she can borrow his sister's helmet and knee and elbow pads. When Olivia gets to Miguel's house, however, she finds that Miguel's sister has loaned her equipment to someone else.

> Sasha and Jasmine have made plans to go hiking together in a national forest. However, the weather report is now predicting thunderstorms and hail for the day of their hike. Jasmine does not think it's safe for them to be outside and far from home in bad weather like that.

> Daniel invites Yoni to go swimming in a section of the lake that has "No Swimming" signs posted. Yoni knows that this part of the lake is known for its sudden drop offs and rocky bottom.

> Answers will vary. Students should show knowledge of refusal skills in their role-plays.
> _____
> _____
> _____
> _____

2. With your partner, discuss how one teen in the role-play will pressure the other. Also, discuss how the other teen will use refusal skills to avoid the unsafe behavior.

3. Together, practice role-playing the situation. Then present your role-play to the rest of the class.

Chapter 21 Study Guide
Environmental Health

> **Study Tips**
> ✔ Read the chapter objectives.
> ✔ Look up any unfamiliar words.
> ✔ Read the questions below before you read the chapter.

As you read the chapter, answer the following questions. Later you can use this guide to review the information in the chapter.

Lesson 1

1. What are some of the major sources of air pollution?

   Most air pollution comes from humans. Sources of air pollution include burning fossil

   fuels, such as oil, coal, and natural gas; chemicals, such as pesticides; and other sources,

   such as forest fires, dust storms, and volcanoes.

2. What are pesticides?

   Pesticides are products used on crops to control insects and other pests.

3. What are some of the effects of air pollution?

   Some of the effects of air pollution include acid rain, smog, destruction of the ozone

   layer, and global warming.

4. What is smog?

   Smog is a yellow-brown haze that forms when sunlight reacts with air pollution.

Chapter 21 Study Guide
Environmental Health

5. What is the ozone layer?

The ozone layer is a shield that protects living things from ultraviolet (UV) radiation.

_____

_____

6. What are hazardous wastes? Name some examples of hazardous wastes.

Hazardous wastes are human-made liquid or solid wastes that may endanger human

health or the environment. Some examples of hazardous wastes include asbestos, lead,

batteries, bleach, insecticides, motor oil, antifreeze, and some cleaning fluids.

_____

_____

_____

Lesson 2

7. What is the Environmental Protection Agency?

The Environmental Protection Agency (EPA) is the governmental agency that is committed

to protecting the environment.

_____

8. What are some ways you can help to keep the air clean?

Answers may include the following: Walk or bike to nearby places. This helps cut down

on air pollution from cars. It will help you to stay active. Use public transportation or

carpool. Riding the bus, subway, or train cuts down on the number of cars on the road.

Don't burn trash, leaves, or brush. Put leaves, grass, newspaper, and food items into a

compost pile.

_____

9. What are nonrenewable resources?

Nonrenewable resources are substances that cannot be replaced once they are used.

_____

Chapter 21

Chapter 21 Study Guide
Environmental Health

10. What is conservation?

Conservation is the saving of resources.

_____

11. What does biodegradable mean?

Biodegradable means that something is broken down easily in the environment.

_____

12. What is precycling, and how can you do this?

Precycling is reducing waste before it occurs. You can do this by buying things that are in

packages you can reuse or recycle, looking for items in containers that you can refill, and

by bringing a cloth bag to the store to carry home your food.

_____

_____

Chapter 21

Activity 88
Use with Chapter 21, Lesson 1

Pollution and Health

Imagine that you are on a quiz show. One of the categories is pollution. The quiz show host presents an answer. You must supply the question.

1. **Answer:** Results from ongoing human activities that release gases, dust, soot, and other substances into the air.

   Question: _What is air pollution?_

2. **Answer:** Burning these releases toxic gases that harm the atmosphere.

   Question: _What are fossil fuels?_

3. **Answer:** Any dirty or harmful substances in the environment.

   Question: _What is pollution?_

4. **Answer:** A yellow-brown haze that forms when sunlight reacts with air pollution.

   Question: _What is smog?_

5. **Answer:** 4.4 pounds.

   Question: _How much solid waste does the average U.S. citizen produce?_

6. **Answer:** Used on crops to control insects and other pests.

   Question: _What are pesticides?_

7. **Answer:** Air pollution intensifies this.

   Question: _What is the greenhouse effect?_

8. **Answer:** Acts as a shield that protects living things from ultraviolet (UV) radiation.

   Question: _What is the ozone layer?_

9. **Answer:** A rise in the earth's temperatures.

   Question: _What is global warming?_

10. **Answer:** Human-made liquid or solid wastes that may endanger human health or the environment.

    Question: _What are hazardous wastes?_

Chapter 2

Activity 89
Use with Chapter 21, Lesson 2

Preventing and Reducing Pollution

Suggest a way to reduce, reuse, or recycle each waste item listed below. Then answer the question that follows. One item has been filled in as an example.

	Plastic Grocery Bag	Glass Pickle Jar	Used White Computer Paper	Out of Fashion Jeans
Reduce	Use cloth bags for grocery shopping.	Buy products in bulk.	Print only when it is necessary.	Do not buy clothes that will go out of style.
Reuse	Use the bags again for carrying anything.	Store leftovers.	Use both sides of the paper.	Keep the jeans and change the style.
Recycle	Use the bags for projects.	Use for storing pens and pencils.	Use as scratch paper for notes.	Donate them to a charity.

What products do you think are worst for the environment? Explain your answer.

The worst products for the environment are those that have a one-time use, like juice boxes

or paper plates.

_____

_____

_____

_____

_____

Chapter 21 (sidebar)

Chapter 21 Health Inventory

How Do You Help the Environment?

Rate your awareness of environmental problems and what you can do to help. For each item below, circle the word that tells how often you behave as described.

Always   Sometimes   Never   **1.** I use reusable materials instead of paper plates and cups.

Always   Sometimes   Never   **2.** I buy in bulk when I can.

Always   Sometimes   Never   **3.** Rather than ride in the car, I walk or ride my bike when I can.

Always   Sometimes   Never   **4.** I use public transportation whenever necessary.

Always   Sometimes   Never   **5.** I turn off radios and TVs when I am not using them.

Always   Sometimes   Never   **6.** I turn down the heat when no one is home.

Always   Sometimes   Never   **7.** I help recycle paper, plastic, aluminum, and glass.

Always   Sometimes   Never   **8.** I do not run the dishwasher or washing machine unless I have a full load.

Always   Sometimes   Never   **9.** I take a reusable plastic bag with me when I shop to hold my purchases.

Always   Sometimes   Never   **10.** I do not leave water running.

Always   Sometimes   Never   **11.** I choose products that are packaged in reusable or recycled packaging.

Always   Sometimes   Never   **12.** I reuse items by repairing them, selling them, or donating them to charity.

Always   Sometimes   Never   **13.** I am willing to volunteer my time to make the environment cleaner and safer.

Always   Sometimes   Never   **14.** I use biodegradable detergents and other products.

Score yourself:

Give yourself three points for each *Always* answer, 1 point for each *Sometimes* answer, and 0 for each *Never* answer. Write your score here.

36–42: Excellent! You are doing your part for a healthy environment.

26–35: Good. You are trying. Keep up the effort.

Fewer than 26: You need to do a better job of protecting the environment. See what you can do to improve. This is the only world we get.

Chapter 21

Academic Vocabulary
Use with Chapter 3

Mental and Emotional Health

Mental and emotional health involves the development of a positive self-concept. Your self-concept is the view that you have of yourself. Finding healthy ways to express feelings and to manage stress helps promote mental and emotional well-being. The following vocabulary words will help you read and talk about issues related to your emotions and your self-concept.

Academic Words That Relate to Mental and Emotional Health		
apparent	identify	react
attitude	mental	source
challenge	psychology	stress

Vocabulary Overview

Read the following list of words and their general definitions. Read the sentences and think about how these words are used to discuss mental and emotional health. Review the words several times to familiarize yourself with their meanings.

apparent (adj.): open to view or clearly seen

Maya's feelings were apparent by the frown on her face.

attitude (n.): a feeling or emotion about something

A positive attitude is an important part of staying healthy.

challenge (n.): a difficult task or problem

Setting realistic goals can be a challenge for many teens trying to build self-esteem.

identify (v.): to name; to make known

It's important to be able to identify the warning signs of emotional disorders.

mental (adj.): having to do with the mind

Schizophrenia is a mental illness in which people lose touch with their real lives.

Academic Vocabulary
Use with Chapter 3

psychology (n.): the study of the mind and behavior of people

Doctors who have studied psychology help people who have emotional problems.

react (v.): to respond; to change behavior

It's important to find healthy ways to react to stress in your life.

relieve (v.): to remove; to take away

You can relieve tiredness by sleeping, stretching, breathing deeply, or resting.

source (n.): the person, place, or thing from which something begins

A source of help for a teen with emotional problems could be a counselor.

stress (n.): the body's response to real or imagined dangers or other life events

Too much stress can cause a person to become ill.

Check Your Understanding

Now that you have reviewed the vocabulary on mental and emotional health, check your understanding by matching each word to the phrase that best describes its meaning.

Words		Definitions
__f__	**1.** apparent	**a.** giving something a name
__d__	**2.** attitude	**b.** a job that is difficult
__b__	**3.** challenge	**c.** the body's response to an imagined fear
__a__	**4.** identify	**d.** a feeling towards something
__e__	**5.** mental	**e.** having to do with the mind
__h__	**6.** psychology	**f.** easy to see
__g__	**7.** react	**g.** to change because of another action
__j__	**8.** relieve	**h.** the science of the mind and behavior
__i__	**9.** source	**i.** the beginning point
__c__	**10.** stress	**j.** to take away

Academic Vocabulary
Use with Chapter 3

Find Related Words

Many words are organized into word families. They are related because they share the same root. Review the related words below. On the lines that follow, try to write five other words that can be added to this list of related words.

apparent
apparently

mental
mentally

source
sources
sourceless

attitude
attitudes
attitudinal

psychology
psychologically

stress
stressful
stressor

challenge
challenged
challenging

react
reaction
reacted

identify
identification
identified

relieve
relieved
relieving

Words will vary, but may include *apparentness, unapparent, attitudinally, challenges,*

identifies, identifying, psychologies, reacting, relieves, unrelieved, and *stressed.*

Using Suffixes

Suffixes can be added to words to make related terms that can be used as different parts of speech. Combine the following words and suffixes to create new words.

Words
apparent
identify
react
mental

Suffixes
-ed
-ive
-ly
-tion

1. _____   5. _____
2. _____   6. _____
3. _____
4. _____

Words will vary but may include *apparentness, unapparent, attitudinally, challenges,*
identifies,identifying, psychologies, reacting, relieves, unrelieved, and *stressed.*

Academic Vocabulary

Use with Chapter 3

Write with Academic Vocabulary

Use at least seven of the following ten words in a paragraph about mental and emotional health. Remember, you can use other versions of the words.

apparent	mental	source
attitude	psychology	stress
challenge	react	
identify	relieve	

Paragraphs will vary, but should demonstrate correct usage of vocabulary words and/or variations of the words. Student writing should also reflect correct spelling, punctuation, and grammar.

_____

_____

_____

_____

_____

_____

_____

_____

Academic Vocabulary
Use with Chapter 18

Disease Prevention

If you practice good hygiene habits, you can limit the number of germs you encounter on a daily basis. This, along with eating healthy foods, getting enough exercise, and sleeping well, can help you prevent disease. The vocabulary words in this lesson will help you read and talk about disease prevention.

Academic Words That Relate to Disease Prevention		
accurate	monitor	respond
detect	reluctance	strategy
environment	research	transmit
initial		

Vocabulary Overview

Read the following list of words and their general definitions. Read the sentences and think about how these words are used to discuss disease prevention. Review the words several times to familiarize yourself with their meanings.

accurate (adj.): exact

We went to the doctor to obtain an accurate diagnosis.

detect (v.): to discover

Once the doctor was able to detect the problem, he was then able to choose the right medicine.

environment (n.): surroundings

Keeping your environment clean lowers the number of germs encountered.

initial (adj.): first

Sandra's initial thought was that she had the flu, but she soon realized it was only a cold.

monitor (v.): to observe

The nurse decided to monitor her patient to be sure that his fever did not return.

reluctance (n.): unwillingness

Matt's reluctance to go to the doctor soon changed when he learned that it would help prevent disease.

Academic Vocabulary
Use with Chapter 18

research (v.): investigate

I decided to research the prevention of heart disease for my class presentation.

respond (v.): react in a favorable way

The doctor told Karie that she would most likely respond to the medicine within 24 hours.

strategy (n.): a plan of action

Washing hands frequently is a good strategy for preventing the spread of germs.

transmit (v.): pass on

When you cough without covering your mouth, you can transmit germs to others around you.

Check Your Understanding

Now that you have reviewed the vocabulary on disease prevention, check your understanding by matching each word to the phrase that best describes its meaning.

	Words	Definitions
__j__	1. accurate	**a.** spread
__d__	2. detect	**b.** surroundings
__b__	3. environment	**c.** the condition of not wanting to do something
__f__	4. initial	**d.** to find out
__e__	5. monitor	**e.** to watch closely
__c__	6. reluctance	**f.** beginning
__i__	7. research	**g.** an action plan
__h__	8. respond	**h.** react positively
__g__	9. strategy	**i.** study
__a__	10. transmit	**j.** correct

Academic Vocabulary
Use with Chapter 18

Find Related Words

Many words can be organized into word families. They are related because they share the same root. Review the related words below. On the lines that follow, try to write five other words that can be added to this list of related words.

detect	**monitor**	**respond**
detectable	monitoring	respondent
detected	monitors	responded

environment	**reluctance**	**transmit**
environmentally	reluctancy	transmittable
		transmitting

initial	**research**
initially	researchable
initialing	researched

Words will vary, but may include *detecting, detects, environmental, environments, initialed,*

initials, monitored, reluctant, researching, researched, researches, responding, responds,

transmitted, transmittance.

Understand Words in Context

Fill in the blanks below with the vocabulary word that best completes the sentence. Make sure you use the correct part of speech and verb tense.

1. Erica _____detected_____ a change in her skin on her left arm.

2. Her _____initial_____ thought was that she shouldn't worry about it.

3. Erica's mother noticed her _____reluctance_____ to go to the doctor to have her skin checked.

4. Her mother _____responded_____ by encouraging Erica to visit their family doctor.

5. Erica agreed that having an expert look at her skin problem was a good _____strategy_____.

6. Erica used the _____library_____ to research possible reasons for the change in her skin.

Academic Vocabulary

Use with Chapter 18

7. She thought that maybe the sun's rays were _____transmitted_____ through the atmosphere to her skin.

8. She had spent most of the summer at the beach, and realized that this was the kind of _____environment_____ that could cause skin damage.

9. The doctor was able to make an _____accurate_____ diagnosis.

10. He said that it was only a minor problem, and thanked Erica for _____monitoring_____ her skin so closely.

Recognize Similar Words

Some words have synonyms, or words that have a similar meaning. Match the words below to their synonyms.

Words		Synonyms
__f__	**1.** accurate	**a.** plan
__d__	**2.** detect	**b.** first
__b__	**3.** initial	**c.** hesitance
__c__	**4.** reluctance	**d.** discover
__e__	**5.** respond	**e.** answer
__a__	**6.** strategy	**f.** correct

Recognize Word Opposites

Some words have opposites, or antonyms. It is as important to understand what a word *doesn't* mean as it is to understand its definition. Match the words below to their antonyms.

Words		Antonyms
__e__	**1.** accurate	**a.** receive
__c__	**2.** detect	**b.** ignore
__d__	**3.** initial	**c.** overlook
__b__	**4.** monitor	**d.** final
__a__	**5.** transmit	**e.** incorrect

Academic Vocabulary
Use with Chapter 18

Write with Academic Vocabulary

Use at least seven of the following ten words in a paragraph about disease prevention. Remember you can use other versions of the words.

accurate	monitor	strategy
detect	reluctance	transmit
environment	research	
initial	respond	

Paragraphs will vary, but should demonstrate correct usage of the vocabulary words and/or

variations of the words. Student writing should also reflect correct spelling, punctuation, and

grammar.

_____

_____

_____

_____

_____

_____

_____

_____

_____

Academic Vocabulary

Injury Prevention and Safety

Paying attention to your surroundings can usually help prevent accidents. When you are aware of safety issues, you are less likely to have injuries. The vocabulary words in this lesson will help you read and talk about injury prevention and safety.

Academic Words That Relate to Injury Prevention and Safety		
appropriate	injure	potential
automate	medical	prohibit
device	minimize	
dispose	occur	

Vocabulary Overview

Read the following list of words and their general definitions. Read the sentences and think about how these words are used to discuss injury prevention and safety. Review the words several times to familiarize yourself with their meanings.

appropriate (adj.): acceptable, suitable for the purpose

Thomas took an appropriate dose of medicine for his age and weight.

automate (v.): work by self-action

There is a machine to automate pumping of the blood when a person's heart has stopped.

device (n.): a piece of equipment designed to perform a certain task

A device called a smoke alarm is used to detect fires.

dispose (v.): to get rid of

After lighting the campfire, Manny made sure the matches were completely out before he went to dispose of them.

injure (v.): hurt

Gloria turned on the light before she went down the stairs so she didn't injure herself.

medical (adj.): relating to the treatment of disease and injury

Severe bleeding requires the help of a medical professional.

Academic Vocabulary
Use with Chapter 20

minimize (v.): make smaller

Jackson always wears a helmet when he rides his bike to minimize the risk of injury.

occur (v.): happen

Fires are less likely to occur if you keep objects that burn easily away from heaters and stoves.

potential (adj.): possible

To avoid potential trouble when I'm out after dark, I always walk with a group of friends in well-lit places.

prohibit (v.): prevent

In Sarah's hometown, there are laws that prohibit skateboarders and bicyclists from riding on the sidewalks.

Check Your Understanding

Now that you have reviewed the vocabulary on injury prevention and safety, check your understanding by matching each word to the phrase that best describes its meaning.

	Words	Definitions
b	1. appropriate	a. throw away
i	2. automate	b. well-suited
d	3. device	c. take place
a	4. dispose	d. a machine for a certain purpose
h	5. injure	e. make less
g	6. medical	f. not allow
e	7. minimize	g. relating to the treatment of illnesses and accidents
c	8. occur	h. harm
j	9. potential	i. work by self-moving
f	10. prohibit	j. capable of becoming real

Academic Vocabulary
Use with Chapter 20

Find Related Words

Words can be built by changing the tense or by adding prefixes or suffixes. Look closely at the words on this list and add two more related words to each. A few have already been completed for you.

Vocabulary Word	Related Word #1	Related Word #2
appropriate	inappropriate	appropriately
automate	automating	
device		
dispose		disposable
injure		
medical		
minimize		minimized
occur		
potential		
prohibit	prohibits	

Answers will vary, but may include *automated, automates, devices, disposed, disposing, injured, injuring, injuries, medically, minimizing, occurring, occurred, potentially, prohibited,* and *prohibiting.*

Choose the Best Word for the Job

To explain your ideas clearly, you need to choose the best word for the job. Read each sentence below and underline the word in parentheses that best completes the sentence.

1. Daniel dressed (appropriate/<u>appropriately</u>) by putting on a hat and gloves before he went out in the snowstorm.

2. The building's (automate/<u>automated</u>) sprinkler system could prevent serious injuries and damage during a fire.

3. There is a (<u>device</u>/devices) that can be used to restore a person's heartbeat when it stops.

4. The nurse wore (dispose/<u>disposable</u>) gloves when she gave me the vaccination.

5. To avoid (injure/<u>injury</u>), always wear seatbelts when traveling in a car, even if traveling a short distance.

Academic Vocabulary

6. Sharon called for (<u>medical</u>/medically) help while I lifted Susana's bleeding arm so that it was above the level of her heart.

7. The workers (minimize/<u>minimized</u>) the risk of injury by keeping boxes clear of the aisle and by cleaning up all spills immediately.

8. When John noticed that the signs of heat exhaustion were (occur/<u>occurring</u>), he decided he should rest and drink water.

9. To avoid (<u>potential</u>/potentially) accidents during a power failure, keep a flashlight readily available.

10. When natural disasters occur, you might be (prohibit/<u>prohibited</u>) from returning to damaged areas until they are deemed safe.

Write with Academic Vocabulary

Use at least seven of the following ten words in a paragraph about injury prevention and safety. Remember you can use other versions of the words.

appropriate	injure	potential
automate	medical	prohibit
device	minimize	
dispose	occur	

Paragraphs will vary but should demonstrate correct usage of vocabulary words and/or variations of the words. Student writing should also reflect correct spelling, punctuation, and grammar.

_____

_____

_____

_____

_____

_____

_____

_____

_____

_____

Academic Vocabulary

Environmental Health

Your environment is made up of all the living and nonliving things that surround you. Pollution can greatly affect air, water, land, plants, and animals. Preventing and reducing pollution is a part of staying healthy. The vocabulary words in this lesson will help you read and talk about environmental health.

Academic Words That Relate to Environmental Health		
bulk	generation	voluntary
cease	impact	widespread
diminish	regulate	
expose	resource	

Vocabulary Overview

Read the following list of words and their general definitions. Read the sentences and think about how these words are used to discuss environmental health. Review the words several times to familiarize yourself with their meanings.

bulk (adj.): large in mass or amount

The bulk coal burned at the factory produced energy, but the soot and ash polluted the environment.

cease (v.): stop

Because there were so many cigarette butts found on the beach, a law was passed that called for everyone to cease smoking at the beach.

diminish (v.): make smaller

To diminish the amount of solid waste material in our landfills, we must recycle.

expose (v.): make known

The newspaper article was written to expose the dangers of water pollution caused by a sewage spill.

generation (n.): the act of producing

The burning of coal and oil causes the generation of chemicals that mix with water in the air to produce acid rain.

Academic Vocabulary

Use with Chapter 21

impact (n.): effect

The recycling program at school has made a big impact by decreasing the amount of paper that is thrown away.

regulate (v.): control

Drew bought a system that would regulate the temperature in the room to save energy.

resource (n.): something that can be used when needed

Oil is a limited energy resource that must be conserved because once we use it, it's gone.

voluntary (adj.): done of one's own choice

We turned off the lights as a voluntary effort to save energy and lower our electric bill.

widespread (adj.): spread over a large area

Sewage spills contribute to the widespread problem of water pollution.

Check Your Understanding

Now that you have reviewed the vocabulary on environmental health, check your understanding by matching each word to the phrase that best describes its meaning.

	Words	Definitions
h	1. bulk	a. an available supply
c	2. cease	b. adjust or manage
f	3. diminish	c. end
d	4. expose	d. reveal
g	5. generation	e. influence
e	6. impact	f. make less
b	7. regulate	g. the act of making something
a	8. resource	h. great amount
j	9. voluntary	i. occurring over a large region
i	10. widespread	j. done willingly

Academic Vocabulary
Use with Chapter 21

Find Related Words

Many words, like the ones in this activity, can be organized into word families. Review the word families below. Write at least one new related word in each box.   Words will vary; some examples are given.

cease ceasing ceased	diminish diminished diminishing	expose exposes exposed
generation generationally generational	impact impacted impacts	regulate deregulated regulated

Understand Words with Multiple Meanings

Some words have more than one meaning. Match the definitions in the boxes to the underlined words in the sentences that follow.

The word *bulk* has three meanings:
a. (adj.): large mass or amount
b. (n.): the greater part of something
c. (v.): to swell or grow in size

___b___ 1. The bulk of the problem is that the large production of waste materials ends up in our rivers and streams.

___a___ 2. Bulk grain could be used to create a cleaner type of fuel for automobiles.

___c___ 3. Rice and grains bulk up in water.

The word *generation* has two meanings:
a. (n.): a group of individuals who are about the same age
b. (n.): the act of producing

___b___ 4. The generation of large amounts of trash has caused the land-fills to swell with garbage.

___a___ 5. The younger generation is learning more about how health is related to the environment.

Academic Vocabulary
Use with Chapter 21

The word *impact* has three meanings:
a. (v.): to have an effect
b. (n.): the striking of one thing against another
c. (n.): effect

___a___ **6.** We hope that the banning of certain chemicals will positively <u>impact</u> the earth by stopping further damage to the ozone layer.

___c___ **7.** The harmful <u>impact</u> of acid rain on plants and aquatic life has lead some people to reduce the amount of fuel they burn.

___b___ **8.** The oil spill was the result of an <u>impact</u> between the tanker and a large rock.

Write with Academic Vocabulary

Use at least seven of the following ten words in a paragraph about environmental health. Remember you can use other versions of the words.

bulk	impact
cease	regulate
diminish	resource
expose	voluntary
generation	widespread

Paragraphs will vary, but should demonstrate correct usage of the vocabulary words and/or variations of the words.

_____

_____

_____

_____

_____

_____

_____

_____

_____

_____

_____